CONTEMPORARY
RESTAURANTS
AND BARS

CONTEMPORARY
RESTAURANTS
AND BARS

MARTIN M. PEGLER

VISUAL REFERENCE PUBLICATIONS, INC. — NEW YORK

Copyright © 2004 by Visual Reference Publications, Inc.

Visual Reference Publications, Inc.
302 Fifth Avenue
New York, NY 10001

Distributors to the trade in the United States and Canada
Watson-Guptill
770 Broadway
New York, NY 10003

Distributors outside of the United States and Canada
HarperCollins International
10 East 53rd Street
New York, NY 10022-5299

Library of Congress Cataloging in Publication Data:
Main entry under title: Contemporary Restaurants and Bars

Printed in China
ISBN 1-58471-046-2

Book design: Dutton & Sherman

CONTENTS

INTRODUCTION

Societies' search for a greater sense of excitement and sizzle in their surroundings is most apparent when people go out to dine and drink.

In Contemporary Restaurants & Bars we bring you the "hot spots" and the "in places" where being there and being seen there are almost as important as the chef, the cuisine and the wine and liquor selection.

Bright lights, vibrant colors, pulsating music and rich materials are combined with unique architectural forms and shapes—with fantasy and flair—and occasionally even a touch of nostalgia and tradition—to satisfy the public's unending appetite for "what's new?"—"where's it at?"—and "what's happening?"

With examples by leading designers and drawn from "in places" around the world, Contemporary Restaurants & Bars presents a lush and brilliant array of designs that are fresh, smart and stylish. The gamut ranges from minimalist sophistication to downright homey. The bars may be stand-alone attractions or annexed to restaurants or lounges and the drink of choice ranges from liquors to fine wines. Whatever—the designs have people clustering around the bars or queuing up for tables in the restaurants.

These spots are hot!

CONTEMPORARY

RESTAURANTS AND BARS

LOEW'S LOBBY RESTAURANT

LOEW'S PHILADELPHIA HOTEL, PHILADELPHIA, PA

INTERIOR ARCHITECTURE & DESIGN —
Daroff Design Inc. + DDI Architects, P.C., Philadelphia, PA
Karen Daroff : Principal in Charge
Martin Komitzky: Principal-Director of Design
Alina Jakubski : Principal-Project Manager

ARCHITECT OF RECORD — *Bower Lewis Thrower Architects*

HISTORIC ARCHITECT — *Powers & Company*

PHOTOGRAPHY — *Peter Paige*

The new Loew's Philadelphia Hotel is located in the landmark 1932 building. Featured in the lobby is the 265-seat restaurant shown here. In keeping with the hotel's "visual theme of quality and timeless modernity," the designers at Daroff Design incorporated details and materials of the 20s and 30s but did not attempt to reproduce any specific historic period.

"Through the use of a warm palette of colors, textures and patterns inspired by Hollywood's cinematic vision of the 1930's, Loew's guests feel the splendor and grace of that era, while enjoying the modern amenities and features." This is

especially felt in the dining room where the physical space is enriched with patterned carpeting, dramatic lighting, ornamental metalwork, carved glass and custom art fixtures. A custom designed mosaic mural inspired by an art deco pattern was commissioned for the feature wall of the dining space.

The elliptical-shaped bar sits beneath a multi-tiered dropped ceiling that restates the ellipse and accentuates the form with a blue wash of light. Curved, arc and oval shapes reappear throughout the design, underscoring the "moderne" and "art deco" inspirations inherent in the design. The same swirling feeling is seen in the patterned carpet with geometric and arced shapes in coral, salmon, gold and blue/violet, inspired by the artwork of Le Corbusier. The rich earthy colors are also used to upholster the chairs in the dining room and the soft lounge furniture inspired by the designs of the 1930's French architect Pierre Chareau. The bar floor, which is an extension of the lobby, is finished with custom blended black terrazzo to match the original existing flooring.

To maintain the look of the building in the public and the guest rooms, the designers created "a consistent visual experience" by incorporating materials used in the original building such as Belgian black, Bandiglio Gray and reddish Numideane Sanguine marbles, juxtaposed with exotic millwork in Sapele Pommele and Makore woods Their design concept was "in adapting this theme from office building to the hotel interior, rich textures, soft colors and art features will soften and enrich the guests' experience." "The international style will enhance and reinforce the building's exterior design and theme" and what was originally the PSFS Bank and Building in 1932, is in this century a warm, welcoming and elegant hotel with a handsome restaurant/lounge/bar.

LACROIX

RITTENHOUSE SQUARE, PHILADELPHIA, PA

DESIGN — *Marguerite Rodgers Ltd., Philadelphia, PA*

PHOTOGRAPHY — *Matt Wargo*

Located in the elegant Rittenhouse Hotel on the very chic Rittenhouse Square in the upscale part of Philadelphia, is the Lacroix Restaurant. Marguerite Rodgers, the designer, met the vision of the famed chef, Jean-Marie Lacroix, and designed "a completely sensory dining experience" to showcase his culinary talents.

"Stone pathways, warm sunlight and abundant greenery capturing the spirit of the elegant park and garden" greet the guests at Lacroix. Flame-tipped candles appear along the vestibule wall and the stone flooring leads past the steel and oak wine display case, exciting cheese and dessert carts, and a "food altar": "an oversized replica of a fountain displaying wines, flowers and culinary delicacies".

Finally—at last—they reach the dining room and the view of the park.

To make the comfortable elegance possible, the platformed dining room was lowered and the ceilings made one height throughout. A glass railing was added " to create more depth, openness and calm." The floor-to-ceiling columns along the length of the room are finished with smooth Venetian plaster and washed in light. In this space's former restaurant an intimate lounge café has replaced what was previously a private dining room. Here, guests can enjoy lounging at chocolate brown leather wrapped tables before sitting down to dinner.

The 110-seat restaurant is warm and gracious in a color scheme of yellows, greens and earth tones. Guests are "enveloped" by the richly textured, upholstered walls and ceiling and the natural Roman shades. The plushy green velvet banquettes, booths and chairs have been designed in the style of the French designer Jean-Michel Frank. Inspiration for the décor also comes from furnishings and interiors of

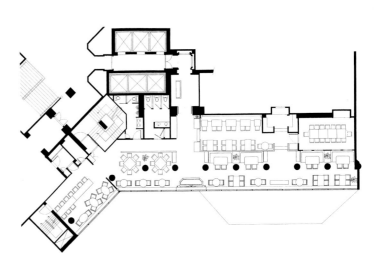

the 30s and 40s as well as garden settings as well as some Asian accents. Directional lighting and custom candle sconces and pendant fixtures softly illuminate the restaurant. At night, candles on the tables create a sense of intimacy and "the illusion of dining by moonlight/" By daylight, the space feels like an open garden.

The refined, contemporary menu is matched by the comfortable elegance of Lacroix: innovative, recognizable, sophisticated and inviting.

The color-infused wine bar/restaurant, Adega, is situated in a corner of the 19th century Union Station in Denver. The design by Semple Brown "respects the original character yet remakes it from within."

A raised stone panel screen wall creates a distinct and sheltered space at the entry. "By affording controlled views of the wine bar, dining room, and the wine room, the entry foreshadows the motifs to be revealed throughout the restaurant." A focal element of the restaurant—and thus of the design—is the extensive wine collection. A freestanding, transparent and elegant glass-enclosed wine room is visible throughout and serves to organize the space.

Complementing the wine room is the dining experience that follows in the dining room. "Through exaggerated columns and suspended ceilings, the existing heavy timber building is veiled from within." The stone panel wall at the entry and the translucent wall of the wine room at the opposite end anchor the space and the shape is reinforced by the undulating ceiling panels that run the length of the room.

The wine bar itself is a collection of smaller and unique spaces with the aforementioned wine room as a background. Here, too, simplicity is the keynote and the cocktail tables

ADEGA

UNION STATION, DENVER, CO

DESIGN — *Semple Brown, Denver, CO*

PHOTOGRAPHY — *Ron Pollard*

1 Entry
2 Bar
3 Dining Room
4 Private Dining Room
5 Wine Room
6 Restrooms
7 Chef's Dining Table
8 Kitchen
9 Patio

are topped with glowing resin blocks as is the backlit resin top of the bar. The darker and lower ceiling panels in the upper lounge "compress the space for a more intimate environment."

Glass, stone, glowing blocks of resin, a fabulous full wall mural, sheer curtains that serve as movable dividers, dark stained wood floors, massive columns and the utter simplicity of design together create the unique look of Adega "A sensibility toward materiality and light bring the sensations of sight and touch to a place focused on the senses of aroma and flavor. The richness and honesty of the materials enhance the contrast between natural and man-made."

ARIA

FAIRMONT HOTEL, CHICAGO, IL

DESIGN — *Marve Copper Design, LLC, Chicago, IL*

MARVE COOPER: *Principal (formerly of Lieber Cooper Associates)*

PHOTOGRAPHY — *Mark Ballogg: Steinkamp Ballogg Photography*

The designer, Marve Cooper, had as an objective to not merely establish a warm, sultry, and sensuous mood but give the restaurant an identity of its own, independent of the hotel's. Thus, Aria has an entrance off the street as well as from the Fairmont Hotel where it is housed. While the Fairmont is adorned with "traditional opulence," Aria's look is distinctly different. When the restaurant opened, it received rave reviews in the local press calling it clean, elegant and the modern elements were described as "pleasantly down to earth."

Cooper gave Aria a strong visual cohesiveness. "Its irregular, angular floor plan and multiple functions are tied together by a curvilinear plan using arc shaped counters and rounded partitions, soffits and ceiling coffers that relate to its graphic identity." Aria's street entry foreshadows the unity of the design that distinguishes the interior. The curved entry fascia opens into the cocktail lounge. Here there are rounded arm seating, circular tables, and an upholstered banquette wall above that is a photomural celebrating music and dance. A series of sweeping circle cut-outs—in the tiered ceiling—serve to encompass and enfold the space while restating the curves and arcs of the walls and the golden half moon motif behind the bar.

"The connections between the rooms are anchored by the circularity at their ends. Arc-shaped lighted ceiling coffers, curved wall sconces, and rounded alcoves diminish the corridor's straightness." Focal in the dining room is the "library wall" of wine. The wine display is glassed in and displays the cylindrical bottle ends. Opposite, the arcing chef's action station and a matching food display area "continue the powerful curvilinear design theme and flow." Marve Cooper believes that the uniqueness of the environment and its being thought of as a coherent, positive experience is what ultimately distinguish a restaurant. "The greatest challenge is to create environments that lead to memorable experiences." Aria is memorable.

FISH OUT OF WATER

WATERCOLOR, FL

DESIGN — *Rockwell Group, New York, NY*

PHOTOGRAPHY — *Paul Warchol*

The "Fish Out of Water" is a cool and refreshing experience—and not at all like a "fish out of water." It couldn't be more safely, securely and pleasantly anchored than it is in Watercolor, FL. As designed by The Rockwell Group, the 4500 sq.ft. restaurant/lounge can seat 180 in the dining room and 25 at the bar.

If you are lucky enough to have to wait for your table, your experience begins with a drink on the mezzanine while

resting on a teak porch swing. Your introduction to the restaurant interior begins with the Ice Bar where an under counter display of fresh seafood/shellfish appears in the stone and glass raw bar. The finishes in the drink bar area include iridescent glass mosaic tiles, a limestone bar top, a frosted mirror back bar accented with "driftwood"-colored shelves for the display of liquor and glasses. The lounge seating in the bar overlooks the main dining room as well as the pool and the gulf beach beyond.

Guests walk down a shallow ramp to get to the main dining room. On one side is a curved salmon/melon colored plaster wall with an opening through which the expo-grill kitchen can be viewed. A "sea-grass" and "sea-pod" railing—a sculptural caprice—is on the opposite side. The color palette here is "very cool, sun-bleached": white plaster walls, sea-grass ceiling coves, cool gray-blue and fresh sharp green upholsteries and sheer white draperies hung from the ceiling.

Posts featuring hand painted lampshades with images of gulf-water fish are complemented by painted chandelier shades with similarly themed artwork. These appear in the dining room over the circular banquettes. Set into niches in the yellow wall are copper wire framed "fish," pin mounted off the wall.

A private dining area features a red and white wine cellar. The walls are filled with the wines that are served in the restaurant. There is a separate cooler room for the white wines that can be entered through a glass door in the wall from the private dining room. "Fish out of water"? No way! This is a fine way to dine—so dive in and enjoy it all.

NINE

THE PALMS, LAS VEGAS, NV

CONCEPT & IMAGE DEVELOPMENT —
Scott de Graff of the Nine Group, LLC and
James Geier of 555 Design Fabrication Management

ARCHITECTURAL & ENVIRONMENTAL
DESIGN — *555 Design Fabrication Management,*
Chicago, IL
James Geier: Principal
Richard N. Marohn, AIA / Karen Herold / Matt Mikyska

CLIENT — *Nine Group, LLC*
Scott de Graff / Michael Morton

PHOTOGRAPHY — *Nine Group LLC*

One of the highlights in the new 35-story resort complex, The Palms in Las Vegas, NV is Nine, a contemporary American steak house. Nine is an off-shoot of the original Nine that opened a few years ago in Chicago and the team of Michael Morton and Scott de Graff are bringing what Conde Nast's *Traveler* magazine dubbed—"one of the newest, hottest and best places to eat in the whole world"— to Vegas and The Palms. For this 12,500 sq. ft. Nine, the concept and image was developed by Scott de Graff of Nine Group working closely with James Geier, the principal of the 555 Design firm.

A two-sided waterfall and glass-enclosed wine room make a spectacular entranceway into the cavernous restaurant. 2500 bottles of wine can be stored in the glassed-in wine room. There they are nestled on 1/2 in. diameter cantilevered pins that protrude from the stainless steel wall panels. The bottles are stacked on stainless and walnut X-bridges suspended from the wall.

A focal point in the dining room is the circular champagne and caviar bar made of walnut and stainless steel. Fiber optic lighting encircles the bar that glows like so many haloes of neon light. A central stepped column of glass and mirrored tiles rises up from the center of the bar and it holds display shelving made of acrylic material. Here, too, fiber optics add a magical touch to the shelf illumination and the display of the champagne bottles. The bar is encircled by 20 low-backed, tubular chrome/stainless steel stools. Like most of the custom elements in Nine, these were created and fabricated by 555. This main dining room can accommodate 175 for seated dinner service or 300 at receptions.

A triple-domed, silver leaf covered ceiling "morphs moods" via a 300-color computerized neon lighting system. The rest of the space is elegantly understated but enhanced by limestone walls, focal areas of mirrored mosaics, and

sleek and sophisticated booths upholstered in ultra suede complemented by the silvery gleam of leather-like covered, ebony painted chairs. In addition to the main dining, 75 guests can sit in the contemporary but comfortable bar/lounge area or up to 60 can be accommodated in the private dining rooms.

In addition to the Chicago-style steaks and chops in the Morton's of Chicago tradition, consultant/chef Michael Komick working with chef Brian Massie has created a vast selection of seafood specialties including shellfish platters, caviar presentations, sashimi and tartars.

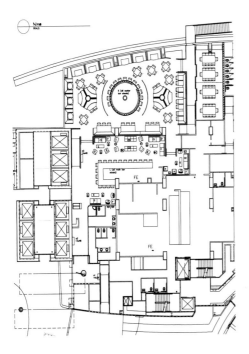

MOD

NO. DAMEN, CHICAGO, IL

DESIGN — *Suhail Design Studio, Chicago, IL*

PHOTOGRAPHY — *Doug Fogelson, www.drfp.com*

"To me, 'mod' represents the abbreviated and hipper side of MOD-ernism," said Suhail, the new, hot, one-named designer on the Chicago scene. "Modernism during the 30s and 40s was all about steel, glass and concrete—it was moving away from decorative ornamentation. This gave me direction and with the name 'MOD' finalized, I felt the interior should convey an homage to the wonderful materials that are available today." His challenge was to take an existing 2700

sq. ft. restaurant and completely rework the space leaving the kitchen in its original location. "Due to the 'organic' nature of the type of cuisine of the proposed restaurant, I felt that I wanted to go completely in the opposite direction with the theme of the design of the space—synthesis."

The motif that Suhail picked for the project was the circle in the square and to emphasize the motif he repeated it over and over again throughout the space. "All the wall and divider panels were jet cut emphasizing the synthetic nature of the concept and the process required to achieve this." For his synthetic palette of materials he selected acrylics, fiber glass, injection molded seats, Corian, recycled plastics, industrial foam, wafer board and stainless steel.

"Mod need not be minimal" and though the restaurant has fashionably clean lines with squared edges, it is filled with articulated details that give the eye plenty to take in such as "the neatly patterned partitions in a variety of eclectic materials, rigorously positioned light fixtures in bold hues, and arresting furnishings which all employ colorful plastic elements fabricated with ejection molding."

Running parallel to the restaurant's dining room is a bold, electric orange entranceway paneled in steel rimmed acrylic squares—some de-bossed with a circle—to create the restaurant's circle-in-the-square logo. A third of the space is devoted to the cocktail lounge where the focal element is the L-shaped stainless steel clad bar. Of the 40 compact fluorescent bulbs used in the ceiling, some are covered with colored gels and wrapped in inflatable plastic shopping bags. Egg-shaped, molded Bombo chairs in green and blue

accompany the Corian-topped tables. Banquettes line one wall and 12 chrome aluminum chairs surround the single communal table. The circle motif appears in the concave marine blue glass pendant fixtures and the convex, safety mirrors on the wall over the banquettes. Recycled tires provide the material for the dove gray inset with sea-green with a terrazzo-look floor.

The dining area is articulated by the screen-style partitions. One set, made of perforated, confetti-colored recycled plastic, separates the bar from the dining room and another, of particleboard, can be used to create a private dining area at the end of the dining room. The rest rooms are hidden behind asteel enameled, orange partition and a translucent corrugated fiberglass screen blocks off the kitchen. "The lively plastic feel of the place is, of course, intentional which allows the simplicity of the 'organic' food served on clean white tableware to be even more appealing." Yes! Mod-ern need not be, and certainly is not, minimal at Mod.

PARAGON RESTAURANT

FOXWOODS RESORT CASINO, MASHANTUCKET, CT

DESIGN COORDINATOR — *Judd Brown Design, Warwick, RI, Judd Brown*

CONCEPTUAL & INTERIOR DESIGN — *New England Design, Inc.*

ARCHITECT OF RECORD — *Jefferson Group Architects, Warwick, RI*

PHOTOGRAPHY — *Warren Jagger*

The "shining jewel" in the Foxwoods Resort Casino is the addition of the new Stargazer Casino and the Paragon Restaurant. In its constant effort to upscale the property and make its amenities more attractive to the special groups of visitors with more affluent tastes and higher gaming ambitions, it was only natural that a gourmet dining experience be added. The Paragon Restaurant, as designed by Judd Brown Design of Warwick, RI, is the answer.

Distinctive and unique architectural elements, and rich and fine finishes, fabrics and materials were used. Throughout, the design is filled with soft and voluptuous curves that arc as in the sweeping circular entrance from the casino, and the gigantic blue and white glass globe of the world that rests on a massive pedestal. Capping the globe—two levels up—is a multi-tiered dome upon which has been

painted a view of a nighttime sky. The globe spins in an open atrium…a cut through of several floors. The dramatic circular base that supports the globe is circled by a sinuously shaped bar that moves around the pedestal. The bar is finished in a striking wood veneer. "We selected unique dramatic veneers and woods to reflect the unique design of the space," said Mark Palazio of JBD Inc. The polyester finish accentuates the richness of the color of the veneer. In addition to its use on the bar, the same rich woodwork appears on the ebony circular columns located throughout the actual dining room. In the dining room the circular motif reappears in the sweeping cut-out troughs that undulate through the room. These openings are highlighted with silver leaf and the artwork, in the raised areas, is illuminated by the hidden cove lighting.

Rich, multicolored marbles in gold, amber, coral, terra cotta and cream—outlined and accented with black—are used in swirling patterns to pave the floor in the bar/lounge. In the dining room the same earthy colors take off in an abstract flowing pattern on the carpeted floor. The brocade-upholstered chairs pick up the burnt orange and bronze-gold colors. Along one almost gold colored wall is a high, camel-back banquette tufted in red orange and gold fabrics that becomes a focal element. Deep blue cloths overlay the tables that are candle lit and accented by mini-spots recessed in the ceiling. Fabric upholstered walls and floor-to-ceiling drapery in patterned damask silks add to the quiet opulence of the space.

For smaller parties there are private dining rooms with diamond tufted walls, cut-out ceilings and dramatically illuminated draperies and ceilings. The high quality look and feel of Paragon has become a prime example of just how fine and upscale the Foxwoods Resort Casino has become.

ZOLA

WASHINGTON, DC

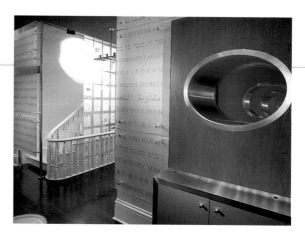

DESIGN — *Adamstein & Demetriou Architects,*
Washington, DC
Olvia Demetriou, FAIA & Theo Adamstein,
Principals in Charge
Ira Tattelman, AIA: Project Manager / Designer
Stacey West: Interior Designer
Team: Caroline Umpjlett / Griz Dwight /
Damian Parsons / Leah White

PHOTOGRAPHY — *Maxwell MacKenzie*

New on the Washington scene—but certainly at home—is the International Spy Museum on F St., NW. The people who run the museum required a 7700 sq. ft. restaurant/bar that could accommodate 175 seated guests and 40 more in a private dining facility. "The client's wishes were for us to draw on the 'shadow world' of espionage (with its mystery, intrigue, disguise, secrecy and danger), but to reflect the world with a non-thematic, subtle design approach." Since the restaurant would be situated in an historic landmark building (the first office building built in Washington during the 19th century), it posed many additional challenges. The architects/designers took great care to preserve and restore details such as the staircases, the room sizes and woodwork, and to allow the existing structures to co-exist and "peak through to the new interventions." Openings within the ancient walls were limited due to the stringent historic preservation requirements and "were expressed through a series of portals."

"The play of masking and unmasking layers of history provided us with a conceptual link to espionage and concepts of transparency, illusion, concealment, information and discovery. We incorporated 'art installations' to tie in with spy references. Oversize glass and acrylic panels with 'ghosted' texts from de-classified CIA and KGB documents and panels with screened images from the world of film noir convey the mysterious world of espionage. These photo graphic panels were used to close off original doorways—allowing for a new circulation pattern and highlight the historic openings."

Flanked by "historic" windows on two sides, the bar/lounge is a large dramatic space with a series of text carved, back-lit wall niches. Also introduced here is the palette of materials and colors that are used throughout: ebony and cherry woods, satin and polished steel, mirrors, etched glass, sumptuous velvets and graphite toned materials. They "come together to create a mysterious but evocative mood."

Open ovals are cut through six of the high-backed, deep red velvet colored booths in the dining room—"reminiscent of luxurious train parlors"—so that guests can sneak a peek into other dining alcoves. The neutral colored walls are complemented by the rich, dark ebony frames and moldings. Oval pendant lamps in the center of each dining room have circuitry embedded in the glass "which in a subtle way refers to communications and 'embedded' secret messages." The lighting fixtures in glass and chrome provide a sleek, refined look while enhancing the sense of mystery. Hidden lighting illuminates both the glass and acrylic panels that enhance the open and inviting ambiance. "The entire effect is one of excitement and intrigue."

TRU

DESIGN — *The Johnson Studio, Atlanta, GA*

PHOTOGRAPHY — *Mark Ballogg, Steinkamp Ballogg Photography*

Lettuce Entertain You Enterprises has parented many successful dining establishments in Chicago and elsewhere, but the elegant, refined TrU is the ultimate "experience." Bill Johnson, the designer of TrU says, "The restaurant is intended to be a gallery—primarily for the culinary art—but for visual art as well." Chefs Gale Gand and Rick Tramento provide the spec-

tacular food while the cool space has 15 ft. ceilings and large wall areas upon which selected artworks are featured.

Past the gracious, dimly-lit entry the guests enter into the high and bright white bar/lounge and the staircase that leads to another lounge in the mezzanine. The back-lit back bar soars up to the high ceiling though only the lower shelves are within reach and functional. The sweeping arc of the bar serves to bring the patrons into TrU and the dining room on the right. The rich blue upholstery and carpeting is introduced here and these continue in the main dining room.

Two sides of the formal dining room are filled with floor-to-ceiling windows that are covered with backlit sheer draperies. A 5 ft. diameter, massive column stands in the geometric center of the room. "The entire space is painted white—like a gallery—with understated upholstery for softness." The space is "intentionally minimalist so that the

focus remains on the food and the chef's presentations. As in a 'gallery'—the focus should always be the art." Though the kitchen is partially visible from the dining room, "The presence of the kitchen is not forgotten and guests can sense the intense effort involved in the preparation of the dishes." This heightens the senses and the anticipation of what is to come. From a design standpoint, both rooms are designed to be minimal but beautiful and perfectly suited to their function. The 3500 sq. ft. restaurant seats 112 in this main room and the private dining area can accommodate 72 more.

Adding a sense of "graciousness" is the open space around the tables and the larger than usual circulation areas. The tables are also larger and the chairs roomier and "more

plush." The high intensity, narrow focus halogen spots are set into the ceiling to dramatize as well as highlight the artwork and the culinary presentations on the all-white tables. These AR111 (4 degree super-spots) "create intense light where they are aimed and contrasting shadows and lowlights where they are not." The private dining rooms—the wine rooms—are not only relatively small but have very low ceilings at 7 ft. 6 in. "It was decided that the display of wine would add warmth and visual interest—creating a cozy, wine cellar-like space."

"TrU is an extremely contemporary space and strives to create luxury in a minimalist way. The space is young, nontraditional, and a fresh approach to high-end dining."

NOVELTY

PHILADELPHIA, PA

DESIGN — *DAS Architects, Philadelphia, PA*
David A. Schultz, AIA & Susan M. Davidson, IDC

PHOTOGRAPHY — *Barry Halkin*

Novelty, the 120-seat restaurant, is snugly enveloped in a turn-of-the-last century industrial building on South Third St. in Philadelphia. It is a welcome addition to the revitalization of the Old City neighborhood which is now home to art galleries and festive nightlife.

The design by DAS Architects of Philadelphia, features the originals and "antique" details of the building such as an elevator gate, exposed pipes, brickwork and a sprinkler hose. The cast iron columns that appear throughout and the distressed plaster and bead board walls and wainscoting, are treated with a multicolor glaze of amber, olive and brown. The original tin ceiling has been restored and by adding strategically placed acoustic panels to the ceiling, the sound level is comfortable and conversation is possible. The floors are finished with planks of American walnut and the carpeting in the rear dining area is a geometric woven pattern in brown, black and taupe.

Following the wishes of the restaurateur, Bruce Cooper, various seating options for 82 guests are available in Novelty's dining area. They range from booths and banquettes to freestanding tables and chairs. The chairs have woven leatherbacks and coffee colored leather upholstered seats. Some of the curving banquettes are finished with a DAS designed small leaf print of black on beige. Other seating is covered in dark mocha leather. Concealed lighting "grazes the tin coffers and highlights textures of the original tin ceiling." Ten customized, industrial-style light pendants with custom rice paper shades give the room a warm glow.

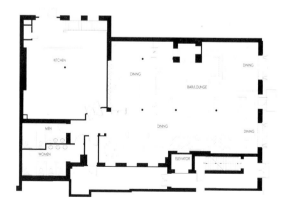

In addition, each table is individually top-lit with low voltage, mono-point fixtures. Adding to the "look" of Novelty are the striking etched metal sculptured wall plaques by Robert Roesch that are "seamlessly incorporated into the restaurant's design."

In addition to the 15-seat bar—voted "Best Bar Scene" by a local publication—with its brushed zinc bar top and walnut veneer face, there is a 38-seat café area up front. This space is further enhanced by two large windows that can open out and a few choice tables where—weather permitting—guests can sit out and mingle with the hip crowd walking by.

56 WEST

CHICAGO, IL

DESIGN — *Aria Group Architects, Chicago, IL*
Thomas Smiciklas: Principal in Charge
Dan Bern & Pam Harris

PHOTOGRAPHY — *Mark Ballogg: Steinkamp Ballogg,*
Photography, Chicago, IL

Reminiscent of a bygone era in Chicago when three knocks on a door in a back alley and the right password gained one entrance, 56 West has the mystery and charm of the past—updated.

A custom winding staircase of "rusty" steel leads guests down to the below street level bar/dance club/restaurant on West Illinois in downtown Chicago. The faux finished cement walls are atmospherically rendered to enhance the feeling of age and the exposed concrete ceiling and the pipes and vents—all painted and antiqued in grays—furthers that image. The deep gray tile floors at the entranceway yield to aged, deep brown timber floors for dancing and dining.

The window-less space is enriched with make-believe window frames and ledges and with glass-framed doors as well as a giant mirror in the bar lounge that also tends to open up the space. The dance floor is located on the elevated bar/dining area that is furnished with a circular, upholstered seating unit in brown, mulberry and taupe velvet, and banquettes covered in black. The elongated glowing onyx community table stands below this area. Giving this basement-level restaurant a unique, one-of-a-kind ambiance are the plush velvets, aged wood floors and the candle-lit, concrete walls that are accented with framed artwork and red velvet draperies. At the far end of the dining room with its rounded booths, upholstered in brown leather with small standing lamps separating the booths, is a brick fireplace. It is set against an aqua tinted wall and flanked by doors leading to the wine storage areas—visible through the glass panes. Throughout, candles in votive glasses, wrought iron candleholders, candelabras and stacked in wood stands near the entrance, promise and fulfill the feeling of mystery and romance at 56 West.

CITY HALL

NEW YORK, NY

DESIGN — *Bogdanow Partners, Architects, PC., New York, NY*

DESIGN TEAM — *Warren Ashworth / Larry Bogdanow / Randi Halpern / Rachel Wilensky*

PHOTOGRAPHY — *Peter Aaron*

Located in the historic Tribeca area, City Hall isn't that far from New York City's real City Hall. The restaurant is in a landmark, 1863 building with original cast iron columns and the façade and entrance lobby have been kept intact. The Corinthian columns that appear out on the front introduce "a visual element that repeats inside." The entrance features a

travertine floor, cast iron columns and high ceilings. From here the guest can pass through formal glass doors into the main dining room—or pass the presentation of fresh fish and seafood on display for the Oyster Bar—or head to the Back Bar. Down the steps are the Vault Room and the Wine Room.

Cast iron columns frame the zinc and American walnut bar in the Back Bar. A custom designed wine rack, also of walnut, is behind the bar and features bottles of red wine. Lending a sense of history to an already historical scene is the exposed brick wall and the pale, silvery fabric on the adjacent banquettes that contrast with the bricks. At the rear of the area is a skylight and beneath it a bluestone staircase with an ornate steel and hardwood railing.

Most of the 1800 sq. ft. street-level floor, with its 15 ft. high ceilings, is devoted to the main dining room. The high-

lights of this space are the Carlisle-style banquettes and the cozy booths around the perimeter upholstered in patterned fabrics in black, gold and burgundy. Ten hanging light fixtures of blackened steel "add drama and contribute a sense of proportion." Enlarged and backlit black and white photographs of New York City in the 20s, 30s and 40s are "evocative—both nostalgic and high style."

Again, in the Vault Room, the drama is in the ceiling which has been opened to expose the original exterior sidewalk glass at the edge of the building line, and the original beautifully-bricked vaults literally under the street. All this is in addition to the original cast iron columns in place.

Bogdanow Partners used "the most and the best of this magnificent landmark building to create a new urban interior out of classic components."

BROADWAY ROOM

ROSIE O'GRADY'S, NEW YORK, NY

DESIGN — *Tree House Design Ltd., New York, NY*
Julius S. "Jack" Baum / John van der Linden

PHOTOGRAPHY — *Stephan J. Carr, New York, NY*

A long established and popular landmark in New York's theater district is Rosie O'Grady's, the American ideal of an Irish pub. When space beneath this restaurant opened up, the owners of Rosie O'Grady's took it and turned it over to Jack Baum of Tree House Design to create a new extension.

Guests can opt, at the entrance, to enter either the original O'Grady''s or to go downstairs to the new Broadway Room. At the bottom of the light-flooded stairwell is a small, carpeted lounge area with upholstered sofas and

lounge chairs arranged around a blazing gas fireplace. The mantel is finished in mahogany and hand painted, glazed tiles. It is topped with a beveled mirror in a mahogany frame. A 30 ft. long mahogany bar is to the right of this area and is set in a field of patterned and multi-colored quarry tiles. Traditional brass and green glass library lamps stand on the bar top to counteract the low ceiling height at this point. A traditional Victorian-style carpet focuses a small dining area across from the bar with its walnut schoolhouse style chairs and white table cloth covered tables.

Throughout the main dining room the designers have evoked a "dignified and tailored English-cum-Irish club room" ambiance through the inclusion of raised wood paneled walls, brass sconces and oil paintings in ornate gilt frames. Embossed tin ceilings, painted with high gloss paint, cover the low ceilings and the area is broken up into bays. These bays are emphasized by tall, thin crown moldings and decorative ceiling-mounted lighting fixtures with antique bronze bodies and hand blown, art glass shades. "The fixtures cast a very warm glow over the entire room and act as a dismembered chandelier as they spread throughout the space."

A room completely finished in mahogany and glass French doors is situated near the bar and it can serve either for private functions or as an auxiliary bar/dining space. "The illuminated vitrines here act as 'windows' and are filled with Irish antiques—such as an Irish grandmother's china cabinet. This partition and vitrines help to dispel the paradox of being underground and create the spirit of a light-filled room at a higher level."

Though the Broadway Room is only steps away from The Great White Way, the artwork and collection of antique music sheet jackets of yesteryear's Broadway musicals make a direct connection with the history of the neighborhood.

What Britney Spears wants—Britney Spears gets—especially when it's a restaurant/bar/lounge designed by Haverson Architecture and Design of Greenwich, CT. With its own entrance on E. 41st St. in New York's Dylan Hotel—under a sweeping serpentine-shape steel and glass canopy one enters Nyla. The entry hall "is an intense chromatic experience" with gold, peach, lavender, pink, deep purple and lime green color-fully-illuminated vaulted niches cut out of the wall on either side of the hall. "Fabric sinuously curves overhead along the ceiling to soften the hard edges and introduce the rainbow of colors of the main dining restaurant space beyond."

Over the rainbow—at the threshold of the entry—is the grand staircase: a transparent design painted in gold/bronze with stainless steel checker plate treads and landings. These lead to a sandblasted, glass floored bridge over to the mezzanine. The stair and the bridge have a mesh guardrail and "the floor glows from cold cathode lighting below" and invites guests across where there is additional seating and a separate bar. A DJ in a control booth is on the first landing. On the way to the upper dining and bar areas, guests get a panoramic view of the ceiling fabric, the bar scene and the seating below, as well as the upper tier of dining booths.

Vintage mahogany wall paneling, an ornate coffered plaster ceiling and a magnificent super scaled fireplace are all part

NYLA

DYLAN HOTEL, NEW YORK, NY

DESIGN — *Haverson Architecture & Design, Greenwich, CT*

PHOTOGRAPHY — *Peter Paige*

of the main dining room which once served as a social hall of the original Chemist's Club. The crowning feature of the room is "a sprightly and architecturally defining 14 ft. diameter chandelier." For Haverson, the challenge was to take these "wonderful artifacts" and use them to their best advantage. Mango, cranberry and violet hues were used to affect a soft and feminine look in the space while still taking advantage of the "dramatic potential" of the space. The chandelier creates a central focus uplighting the ceiling and providing a warm glow to the tables and bar below. "To energize the space, a swirl of sheer, multi-colored fabric moves throughout the room, ascending, twisting, billowing and swagging to become curtains, wall hangings, column wraps and draperies. The ele-

ment is theatrical and full of color—a feminine touch that contrasts the heavy masculine décor of the original 'for men only' room," says the architect/designer, Jay Haverson.

The banquette seating helps to create defined areas for more intimate dining experiences. Half round shapes in banana yellow and tangerine are set next to one another either along the walls or freestanding in the middle of the floor. "Clearly this is a restaurant where seeing and being seen is an important feature but these banquette 'nests' make for a cozy way to relax and be with friends." The space has been designed to encourage and facilitate a feeling of fun through the lighting, the colors, comfortable seating, video presentations, music—and the architectural forms.

STUMP'S SUPPER CLUB

TAMPA, FL

ARCHITECTURE & DESIGN — *Aumiller Youngquist, PC, Chicago, IL*
Raymond R. Schaefer, AIA: Principal in Charge
Mathew Baron: Job Captain

PHOTOGRAPHY — *Mark Ballogg, Steinkamp Ballogg Photography, Chicago, IL*

In addition to being a restaurant, Stump's Supper Club in Tampa, FL also serves as a nightclub and live music venue. The inception of Stump's began when the owners were look-ing to have a restaurant with a viable bar component and—at the same time—looking for a live music venue that had a viable food component. As designed by Aumiller Youngquist of Chicago, they now have a triple threat—an all-in-one club.

Flashing neon signs activate the façade and guests enter past a "lunch counter" which transforms into a full service bar at night. The "merchandising areas" show off Stump's selection of pies, cakes and desserts. Other areas of the 8400 sq. ft. space are "modeled by rooms of a house and feature a living room as well as a recreation room." The rec room has bowling trophies and mementos of a make-believe family

that travels and collects knick-knacks and kitschy items as they go. However, the design team actually did collect the decorative items as well as the lighting fixtures as they set out on foraging excursions in central Florida.

According to the layout, the dinner seating radiates from the stage. It is the focal point in the design. After 9 PM, the dining seats that surround the stage are removed and a dance floor is formed in the center. Surrounding the stage and the impromptu dance floor are more intimate dining "rooms" which have a view of the activity but maintain their own identities. "The best way to sum up the décor and the ambiance of Stump's is to revisit your own Aunt Margie's basement. One is sure to spot a velvet Elvis, string art, shabby lamp shades and even a snow globe or two from Niagara Falls."

Stump's is the alternative for the 25 to 50 crowd who want to venture out but not go to the trendy dance clubs. Here the bands play music from the 60s, 70s, and 80s while customers enjoy a high quality food experience that features Southern style cuisine such as Southern Caviar (pimento cheese spread on crackers) and real filet. Stump's is moving out—next stop—Chicago? Las Vegas? It fills the bill for comfort-food dining, dancing and just listening to music.

AIX

DESIGN — *Etienne Coffinier, covered lampshades, black lacquered louvered finier, Paris, France*

OWNER/CLIENT — *Philip Kirsh*

PHOTOGRAPHY — *Fred Charles, New York, NY*

The designer, Etienne Coffinier of Paris brings "the soul of Provence" to upper Broadway in New York where it complements and visually enhances the cuisine of the acclaimed chef Didier Verot. "The original design of Aix is unlike any-thing New Yorkers have seen before, with a bold design and luminescent colors that evoke the unrivaled emotion and romance of Aix en Provence."

The bi-level dining area can seat 120 guests. Mirrors, louvers and sheer fabric panels play up the brilliant colors of Provence: the almond green and saffron colored fields, the

brilliant orange of the sun, the fiery reds of tomatoes and poppies and berries, and all this glowing under a clear azure blue sky. The dining area is dominated by sweeping, curved red and orange upholstered banquettes and illuminated by hanging fabric-covered lampshades. Black lacquered louvered panels serve as light and sight diffusing partitions throughout, and the dramatic black accent color accentuates the red and orange leather covered chairs. Sheer fabric panels cover the windows of the upper level dining room and they are decorated with a pattern of squares—to "draw in the diffused light."

On the lower level—street level—there is a 40-seat café/lounge/bar that features the artwork of Paul Moran "whose paintings emit a haunting quality evoking familiar yet not wholly identifiable landscapes."

DB BISTRO MODERNE

NEW YORK, NY

DESIGN — *Jeffrey Beers International, New York, NY*
Jeffrey Beers: Principal
Jae Lee / Tim Schollaert: Senior Designers
Martin Wegner: Project Manager
Michelle Buancardo / Lisa Sinclair: FF&E

PHOTOGRAPHY — *Daniel Aubry*

"I wanted to do a bistro that feels French but isn't tradition-al," said master chef and restaurateur Daniel Boulud. Because I come from Lyons, people expected a classic restau-rant, but this is my contemporary interpretation of that style, which is why we added 'moderne' to the name."

It took the talents of Jeffrey Beers to interpret and visu-alize Boulud's feeling and the DB Bistro Moderne is the con-temporary reinterpretation of the traditional European Bistro. Two dining rooms are linked by a paneled wine tast-ing bar that also connects the restaurant to the adjacent hotel lobby. Deep red rubbed plaster walls, two-toned stone tiled floors and a Wenge wood-paneled ceiling distinguish the more casual of the two dining areas. Oversized mirrors in blackened steel frames reflect the "intensely sensual, larger than life" floral photographs by Christopher Beane that adorn the opposite wall. The sculptural modern chairs and tables were inspired by carved African forms. Throughout, the forms and the palette of colors and materials are intend-ed "to recall the European Modernism of the 1910s and 20s." According to Beers, "We wanted this room to be bold-er, edgier. No tablecloths. Plaster walls. Everything with more punch."

The wine bar between the dining spaces is defined by a series of cream-colored arches. The wall opposite holds a wine display "which glows behind its amber colored glass backing." Screening the bar on the hotel facing side of this room are decorative translucent glass window panels with bronze bead curtains. "Putting the bar and the maitre d' stand in the center of the restaurant was intended to force the guests to immerse themselves in the experience. You're jumping right into the restaurant and are in the middle of the chaos that's part of the fun of going to the bistro."

Daniel Boulud said, "It's like the DB hamburger: simple but with an extra complexity. Jeffrey Beers has created a warm, inviting space that is beautiful and at the same time practical."

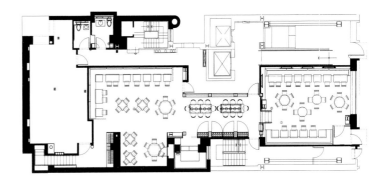

JOEL

ATLANTA, GA

DESIGN — *The Johnson Studio, Bill Johnson*

PHOTOGRAPHY — *Chipp Jamison, Atlanta, GA*

Joel—the name says it all! For those in the "know," Joel is Joel Antunes—a world renowned chef who combines his French traditions with Asian refinements that he picked up while working as the head chef in the elegant Oriental Hotel

in Bangkok. This is HIS restaurant and thus Bill Johnson of the Johnson Studio–the designer of this 12,000 sq. ft. space—knew the design had to be clean and simple. "The challenge of this project was definitely holding back," and, therefore, match the chef's understated style.

This is a clean, open, brasserie-style layout with high ceilings and windows. The lights are recessed in the 16 ft. foot ceilings and in long narrow slots in the walls. According to the designer, "a predominantly white space with intricate details and a spare use of color." The bar is a dramatic element. It is long—like the space—and can seat 65. The focal feature here is the surfboard-shaped, 25 ft. long central table surface where people can gather. Unusual art glass, and upright lighting fixtures highlight the table and echo the motif of the glass insets in the walls. Along the wall opposite the bar are upholstered booths covered in a light, neutral material and red art glass lamps hang down over the individual booths.

In the dining room the high-backed banquettes line the long walls and they are separated by an occasional pier. The high backs are upholstered checkerboard fashion in gentle muted tones of gray, brown, beige and pale gold. In sharp contrast to the rest of the room is the fiery persimmon-color tiled wall that emphatically separates the dining area from the kitchen. Though the kitchen is the "heart" of the restaurant, Joel Antunes wanted it hidden and apart. The dining room can accommodate 128 guests. In addition there is a wine room and an adjacent dining room with a limestone

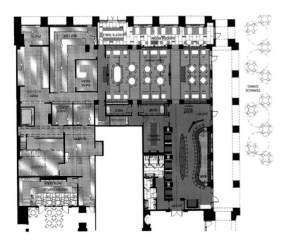

floor and an arched ceiling called the Garden Room. Throughout, the designer specified wood floors accented with deeper colored wood borders and stripes.

Joel has already been named "one of the best restaurants" by *Gourmet* magazine and *Esquire*. The "clean and sleek" look works with Joel's concept of a "chic French brasserie with Mediterranean and Asian influences."

Hotel Monaco on 8th St., SW in Washington, DC is now a boutique hotel that houses the new Poste Restaurant. Originally, back in the 19th century, this historic structure served as the first post office building in Washington. According to the architects/designers, Adamstein & Demetriou, "Our clients' program and goals required an expansion of the original building footprint to accommodate a dramatic entry with bar within a new glass pavilion, an open kitchen, and dining hall and private spaces. Our goal was to create an exciting, contemporary brasserie that would give life to this beautiful building and to create a desirable amenity in a once abandoned courtyard."

The new additions were created "as a contemporary extrusion of the original design." Though the designers took their inspiration from the "historic context"—"Our design had to have a rich, timeless and independent identity." The entrance to Poste is through the historic carriageway portal and the courtyard so the glass and steel pavilion, which contains the bar, is set on this axis so as to be seen from the street. It suggests the old "mail sorting room" and the three portals of the original structure have been mirrored into the pavilion itself "while a trellis-work, metal skin captures the rhythm and scale of the stone coursing."

POSTE

HOTEL MONACO, WASHINGTON, DC

DESIGN — *Adamstein & Demetriou Architects, Washington, DC*
Olvia Demetrious, FAIA / Theo Adamstein: Principals & Designers
Griz Dwight, AIA: Project Manager
Stacey West: Interior Designer
Steve Dickens: Project Architect, Initial phase

PHOTOGRAPHY — *Maxwell MacKenzie*

By contrasting the new against the original shell, the designers were able to insert a functioning kitchen, bar, public and private dining rooms—all into the great room—without carving up the volume of the space. The kitchen was designed as "furniture" like the old dark wood display cases of a past period or a giant "breakfront" or china cabinet. The kitchen, back bar, raised booth seating as well as the custom pendants and cable lights "were designed as elements that would exist independently from the his-

toric space, but would create a dialogue between old and new." For the palette of colors and materials the designers selected patterned velvets for the booths' back upholstery to "provide richness and luminosity and contrast against gold granites." Chocolate brown mahogany and golden Anigre woods were combined with satin metals and large mirrors in a mostly neutral setting; all to achieve the feeling of "a contemporary and reduced interpretation of a traditional brasserie."

BRASSERIE VERT

HOLLYWOOD & HIGHLAND CENTER, BEVERLY HILLS, CA

DESIGN — *Engstrom Design Group, San Rafael, CA*
Jennifer Hohanson, AIA: Principal
Tim Dixon: Project Manager
Tiyanuch Thamchariyawat: Designer
Teresa Purves: Interior Designer

ARCHITECT OF RECORD — *Hayashida Architects*

PHOTOGRAPHY — *Cesar Rubio*

The world famous chef/restaurateur Wolfgang Puck, broke new ground with Brasserie Vert which opened in Beverly Hills, CA. As designed by the Engstrom Design Group of San Rafael, the over 7000 sq. ft. space combines elements of a French bistro/brasserie with an Italian taverna and overlays the new and contemporary with design elements and materials of the past. "We have created a concept that we've never presented before—a marriage of informality and sophistication, modernity and tradition, old and new, that we feel fits into the dynamism of the new century," says Carl Schuster, a partner in Vert and president of Wolfgang Puck Catering & Events.

The shell of the space is new but seems to have been where it is for many years. Jennifer Johanson of the design firm said, "Europeans live with the duality of new interiors dropped into old buildings every day." To create the illusion of age, soft plaster walls, aged barn wood ceilings, faux stone and concrete floors were used.

These contrast sharply with the vivid red Italian chrome chairs in the saffron-colored dining area, the brilliant green (vert) of the bar front panels and the banquettes covered in quilted, electric blue, metallic vinyl fabric.

The bar scene is a "scene." The large communal bar is topped with zinc and between the bar and the lounge, 83 can be seated. Add to this the layered graphic images of "Euro pop" imagery and you have "the hologram-like appearance of a moving party scene." While the daily menu hand written with grease pencil harkens back to the classic French brasserie concept, the assorted colored glass "bottles" of the light fixtures reach back to the Italian roots of the taverna. The glazed wooden doors that can be folded back, open up the bar/lounge and bring the outside inside.

A set of glass doors also open up to the dining room beyond which can accommodate 84. In the warm yellow and red ambiance the focal point is the open stainless kitchen framed by a fiery antique Venetian mirror around the zig-zag opening. The state-of-the-art wood-burning grill allows the chefs/partners—Lee Hefter and Matt Bencivenga—to turn out unique interpretations of brasserie-style cuisine. Dining at Vert is not only colorful but it is a sophisticated dining experience.

MORO

DESIGN — *DAS Architects, Philadelphia, PA*
David Schultz, AIA / Susan Davidson, IDC

PHOTOGRAPHY — *Barry Halkin*

The design inspiration for Moro—which is Italian for the "blood orange"–was fruit! When sliced, the colors, shapes and textures inside the blood orange became the palette for this warm and inviting 100-seat restaurant in Wilmington, DE. DAS, the Philadelphia-based architectural design firm, created small and intimate dining areas with their own identities within the two-story building. They also took advantage of the layout and used glass panels and rounded partitions "to create several different dining environs—unusual for a restaurant."

Textured and patterned fabrics add an "artistic flair" to the dining areas and they are complemented by the dark-stained cherry wood—"to match the natural tones found in the bark of the moro tree." Softly illuminated wine cabinets of cherry wood serve as an entry to the bar/lounge as well as a focal element for the dining room on the second floor. In the various seating areas different lights are used—" reflecting the amorphous moro shapes." Intimate dining is reinforced by these lights suspended over each table, booth or banquette. Some of the fixtures are soft, organic shapes of hand blown glass and others are "oversized—with striking style."

The white and stainless steel kitchen of chef/owner Michael DiBianca is a focal element in the design. DiBianca was very much involved in the evolution of the total design. "For Mediterranean flair," the designers incorporated "red, sun-kissed orange and tangerine tiles" in the exposed areas. The visible wood-burning oven is faced with a mosaic of cracked tiles of the same brilliant colors.

The small bar/lounge is located on the second level and the 12-seat bar is accentuated by the custom millwork that includes hand carved wood panels dyed with a red/orange aniline dye. Red, hand blown, droplet lamps flank the edge of the bar and a "multi-layered" blood orange accent wall envelops the soft furnishings which are covered with an organic print fabric. Moro truly exemplifies DiBianca's vision of "food without boundaries," in a setting rich in color and vitality.

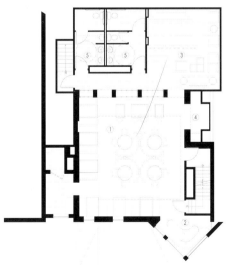

In Italian "fiamma" means "flame" and Jeffrey Beers and his design team drew upon elements and materials native to northern Italy to create this new "hospitality flame" for the New York dining scene. Working for Steve Hanson of B.R. Guest Restaurants, Beers transformed a very narrow, Soho townhouse into a contemporary Tuscan experience. Working within strict fire stair coding requirements, Fiamma spreads out over two levels and basement of the building and can accommodate 130 guests plus an additional 75 in a private function space. The design includes a glass elevator and a marble staircase.

At the entrance, the solid bubinga wood bar counter is accented by an embossed red leather bar face—patterned after an original Italian hand bag. At the rear of the bar area are three large plasma screens behind a smoked glass wall detailed with an inner layer of gold-colored fabric. Brazilian cherry wood planks in random 4 in. and 6 in. widths cover the floor. In the dining area beyond, on the east wall, Morretti glass wall sconces are mounted on seamless carved, rich gold lacquered panels. The sconces appear on either side of a large beveled mirror in a mahogany frame. Silk shaded, custom pendant lamps hang from the red oak beamed ceiling.

FIAMMA OSTERIA

SOHO, NEW YORK, NY

DESIGN — *Jeffrey Beers International, New York, NY*
Jeffrey Beers: Principal
Jae Lee / Tim Schollaert: Senior Designers
Michael Pandolfi / Sara Luhtala: FF&A
Michelle Biancardo: FF & A and Lighting

PHOTOGRAPHER — *Eric Laignel, Photographer /*
Patricia Patrinejad, Stylist

On the second level, three custom pendants mark off the lounge area with the bar on one side and bench seating along the red-orange, Uroboros art glass surfaced wall. A wine station with a white marble-topped bar and wall panels is located in the center of the room. Accenting the room's southern wall is a zebrawood screen with cut-outs backed up by a distressed antique mirror. In the warm and richly-colored dining area is a collection of Italian artwork that hangs on the Venetian stuccoed walls. Red art glass sconces rest upon the mahogany pillars that frame the bays of artwork. Glass and stone mosaic tiles are embedded in the main ceiling beams and on some of the wall panels. Here the floors are finished with random planks of Brazilian cherry wood.

SAVONA

GULPH HILLS, PA

DESIGN — *DAS Architects, Philadelphia, PA*

PHOTOGRAPHY — *Barry Halkin*

What was formerly an 18th century roadside inn—the epitome of Colonial Americana—has been morphed into something else by the design of DAS Architects of Philadelphia. Today, the 4800 sq. ft. intimate dining experience called Savona has a Mediterranean feeling.

The extensive exterior and interior renovations used a blend of rustic and contemporary materials such as terra cotta tiles, cherry wood millwork, earth-toned fabrics, accents of copper, hand forged iron accessories and decoratives as well as custom lighting and furnishings. The bar/lounge is small and intimate as are most of the spaces in Savona. The bar can seat six around its semi-circular shape and it appears to be wedged into a corner. Instead of the traditional back bar the louver covered windows of the building serve as a background for the display of bottles on shelves fitted between the window frames. Terra cotta tiles and wide leaf greenery add to the Mediterranean illusion.

The beamed ceilings in the dining room are painted with the same warm peach/apricot glowing color and the cherry wood dividers are fitted with panes of rippled glass to separate areas and also back up the banquette seating. A fireplace, set catercorner in the room, adds to the sense of intimacy. 110 guests can be seated in the two dining rooms.

Within the stone walls of the historic basement there is a private dining room where guests are seated around a magnificent oval wood table. In addition to the rustic beams overhead and the floor paved with old bricks, the guests are surrounded by myriad bottles of wine displayed in floor-to-ceiling cases finished in the cherry wood.

The stylish and elegant setting has not only received critical acclaim, but it continues to draw and please diners.

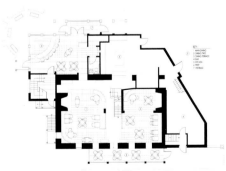

SOLERA

MINNEAPOLIS, MN

DESIGN — *Shea Architects, Minneapolis. MN.*
David A Shea: Principal in Charge
Betsy Gall: Account Manager
Mark Whitenoch: Interior Designer

PHOTOGRAPHY — *Stuart Loren*

"The dining environment isn't just a conduit to the dining experience. It's a part of the experience as important as the flavor of the food and the personality of the servers." Thus, spoke David Shea, principal of Shea Architects and the

designers of the new 4500 sq. ft. Solera restaurant in Minneapolis. The décor and ambiance created by the design team certainly contributes to the success of the Spanish-influenced cuisine of Solera.

For their inspiration, the designers drew on Gaudí's flamboyant and colorful creations in Barcelona. According to the designers, "The design elements in the space utilize materials similar to what Gaudí used: brightly colored mosaic tiles, wrought iron, art glass, etc., but the space is also organic and expressive in a more contemporary, 'modern,' light." The location of the existing kitchen and the bearing walls of the old building determined the rectilinear spaces in the plan. However, "We sought to overlay an organic and rigorous curvilinear quality through the bar, the back bar, booth banquettes and such—and in the floating ceiling element." The custom light fixtures, furniture and sculptural elements also add to the soft, sensuous and sinuous look.

The Tapas Bar is highlighted with broken mosaic ceramic tile medallion insets and the colored mosaic glass tiles used on the curved back bar. Mosaics are used as well on the columns and the host's stand. These materials "relate to the

rich, dark colors of Gaudí's interiors and the cool, sparkling nature of this material is so Mediterranean in feel."

The curved backs of the booths in the dining room "emphasize the overlay of the organic and curvilinear into the rectilinear space." Relating to the reflective glass tiles is the shiny blue striped polyurethane upholstery. This adds to the sparkle already inherent in the metals and lighting used in the space. To compensate for an "awkward" rear space in the dining room, the designers created the Alhambra Room that is partially closed off from the rest of the dining room. It is more Moorish in inspiration with low seating on pillows at lower tables that can be raised to standard height and used with regulation chairs. "The color, light fixtures, fabrics and candles give the room a more intimate and mysterious character." According to Shea, "Everything is part of the dining experience."

DOS CAMINOS

NEW YORK, NY

DESIGN — *Yabu Pushelberg, Toronto, ON*
Glenn Pushelberg / George Yabu
Design Team: Fabienne Moureaux / Andrew Kimber /
Grace Plawinski / Gary Chan
Tech Team: Robert Auger / Shane Park / Karl Travis /
Eric Lam / Catherine Chan

PROJECT MANAGEMENT — *Kevin Storey /*
Christina Gustavs

Two top restaurateurs, Steve Hanson and Jim McDonald, teamed up with Yabu Pushelberg, the Toronto-based design firm, to come up with this exciting new addition to the restaurants lining up on Park Ave. South in New York City.

Dos Caminos is a new look—and has a decidedly new attitude for a South American restaurant.

The emphasis at Dos Caminos is on Central American cuisine served up in a vibrant, exciting and sensory stimulating color scheme of reds and oranges only slightly held in check by a savory chocolate brown. Mole anyone? The large main dining room area combines alcove seating with banquettes and assorted freestanding tables. White gesso covered, metal-sculptured screens serve as dividers between the bench seating to create individual—almost private— booths. The chairs have woven backs and brown leather seats while the banquettes are finished with a brilliant red orange fabric.

DOS CAMINOS
RESTAURANT

YABUPUSHELBERG

The high ceiling has been browned out to disappear. Hanging down from it—in the center of the space—are pierced tree-trunk wood-shaded lighting fixtures that add sharp light accents below as well as diffused light for the tables. Perforated tin lampshades hang down over the side areas of the long room. The walls are plaster textured and are accented with adobe-like brick surfaces. In the main dining room the wall finish is gradated from brown to orange, orange in the transition room, and from orange to pink in the back room. Geometric patterns in brown, beige, cream and red/orange tiles cover the floor.

The bar is finished in a glowing amber color and furnished with leather-upholstered chairs. From the bar, guests can sample over 100 different brands and types of tequila.

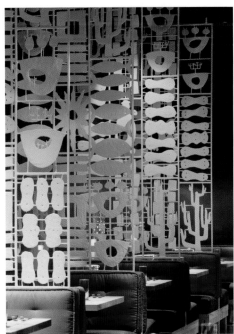

TIERRA DE VINOS

MEXICO CITY, MEXICO

DESIGN — *Groupo Stor, Mexico City, Mexico*
Alfonso Sololoa & Angel Ardisana: Designers

PHOTOGRAPHY — *Luis Gordoa*

Wine is what Tierra de Vinos is all about. The 6380 sq. ft. wine bar/restaurant is located in an old warehouse and as designed by Groupo Stor of Mexico City, the product and the presentation of the product determined the design.

Up front, near the entrance, is the expansive Gourmet Shop where not only is there a wide selection of wines from many countries but also all sorts of wine-related accoutrements for sale. A truly heroic-scaled and curved bar fills most of the space beyond and is the major focus of Tierra de Vinos. The bar also serves to separate the Gourmet Shop from the restaurant area that follows. At the mahogany bar—strong and rustic in styling—the many available wines may be sipped, sampled, savored or drunk. The dark timber floors and the accents of old brick and faux painted stucco all add to the wine-cave ambiance of the bar area.

Under giant, square, alabaster shades—almost like tail-less kites flying overhead—the movable tables and chairs are set out in an amber ambiance. This warm glowing environment is enhanced by the soft color of the walls and the light emanating from the alabaster shades. One wall is dominated by a vast display of wine bottles resting in illuminated wall cases while a tri-part mural by a local artist fills another wall. In Mexican style, the leather back chairs have woven rush seats and the table tops gleam with the highly-finished woods.

MARYSOL

CHICAGO, IL

DESIGN — *Fadesign, Chicago, IL*
Gerardo Fitzgibbon, AIA — Principal & Designer
Design Team — Sanghee Kim / Yuan-ling Ching /
Thomas Kirk / Mary Rigal

PHOTOGRAPHY — *George Lambros,*
Lambros Photography

The new, multi-use/function Marysol is located on W. Randolf St., Chicago's premier restaurant/nighttime/entertainment row. As designed by Gerardo Fitzgibbon of Fadesign—who was in on the project from its inception (he even named it)—Marysol, at times serves as a bar, a tapas lounge, restaurant, live music and dance space or for banquets and private functions.

"The inspiration for the design owes more to the recently published moody photographs of contemporary Cuba by Robert Polidori and Andrew Moore, and to the Modernist design trend, than to the 1940's travel postcard and bongo drum esthetic most of us have come to associate with Cuban entertainment venues. Focusing on a visionary and progressive goal freed us from the obligatory cozy-nostalgic approach and opened the way to explore new possibilities," said Fitzgibbon.

The design was projected "as an architecture of pure color composition—or a modern painting—instead of a series of rooms." In the East room—the heart of the night club function—is the Tapas Lounge and Bar dominated by the undulating bar. Here the design includes a variety of shades and hues of green—suggestive of the sea (the "mar" in Marysol). The greens often contrast in value, intensity and finish "to create a variety of optical illusions meant to play with one's peripheral vision and anchor the various informal arrangements of lounge seating throughout the room." Glowing fluorescent hanging pendants define each of the lounge groups while the floor-to-ceiling draperies accentuate the vertical lines of the interior.

The West room is the more "conventional" dining room but it, too, has been designed to be usable as a dance floor or as a live music lounge. "By design, larger groups of patrons are accommodated by combining various smaller tables around the required circulation aisles. Maintaining axial groupings of

two-tops lighted by a movable cable lighting system sits couples and/or groups of up to 20 guests at once without disturbing other guests." Because all table arrangements are assembled out of smaller tables, banquet seating is easily accommodated as well as is a purer nightclub layout for live music and presentations. Here, orange is the main color; the sun or "sol" in Marysol. Focal points in this room include colored panes of glass "designed to recall the color glazing used in Cuba and to intensify the reflection of the flames emanating from the display kitchen's open grill." Embedded in the east and west wall are aspen wood fiber panels cut out in pie-shaped forms "to create playful figure-ground illusions" that are programmed to change color through a concealed LED system.

"A late night visit to Marysol is a unique nightclub experience offering thorough immersion in Cuban informality, music and attitude"—with food and drink to match.

RUMBA

DESIGN — *Aria Group Architecture, Chicago, IL*

PHOTOGRAPHY — *Doug Snower, Doug Snower Photography*

Aria Group Architects, the Chicago-based design firm, in creating this new restaurant on W. Hubbard in Chicago, sought to capture the essence of a Cuban restaurant with "an authentic old world feel." The plan, as well as the architecture, textures and colors all were selected "to reflect the energy of the Rumba dance."

According to the design team, "Music has harmony that helps unite the space as well as provide a starting point—defined by the stage." They relied on that flow or movement to create the traffic patterns in the dining area. This was established by the seating layout as well as how the servers interact-

ed within the layout. "Music is felt and not seen. The architectural dialogue defines spaces for the music to be enjoyed in different perspectives, from the open general dining seating to the closed, oversized curved booths along the perimeter."

From the long, dark mahogany bar and the soft seating in the brick and stone textured lounge area, the raised stage is visible above a wrought iron balustrade. Old plaster walls; exposed brick piers and herringbone-paved floors are teamed with ruby velour upholstery, ocher gold valances and off-white, floor-to-ceiling drapery.

The natural wood floor in the dining area is a foil for the black lacquered tables and chairs. The cream-colored walls and columns meet the blacked-out ceiling. Along the perimeter wall the swooping, high backed, tufted deep red upholstered arcs enclose individual dining clusters. Along the center of the room, lower, curved banquettes—some anchored to columns—form a partial divider while not actually cutting off views of this space.

The 40-seat private dining room has exposed brick wall areas around the existing old elevator shaft. It provides a dramatic textured highlight to this area with its mini-tile, mosaic floor. Hanging from the dark brown ceiling are atmospheric "candle-lit," antique-style chandeliers. The same creamy color covers most of the walls and some are accented by a wainscot of grayed, robins-egg blue. The dark wood moldings and outlining trim all serve as sharp accents and also enhance the feeling of a quiet dining experience away from the active stage presentation.

FOGO DE CHAO

CHICAGO, IL

DESIGN — *Marve Cooper Design, LLC, Chicago, IL Marve Cooper, Principal (formerly of Lieber Copoper Associates)*

PHOTOGRAPHY — *Mark Ballogg, Steinkamp Ballogg Photography*

Brazil's Fogo de Chao restaurant group was awarded the 2003 "Hot Concept Award" but it is this—the 12,500 sq. ft. Chicago branch—that is the prime example of the chain's focus. As designed by Marve Cooper Design, the 350-seat establishment is "high style and class—dressed up and decked out" and "a departure from big steak houses."

The restaurant follows the Brazilian "churrascaria" concept. It serves simple, flame-cooked meats along with a lavish salad bar. Since this is the lifestyle of the gauchos—Brazilian cattlemen—this represents a rustic and outdoorsy look at life. Marve Cooper selected natural materials: slate flooring, unpainted wood and bare metals—"to capture the simple, straightforward life of the ranchers, while 'civilizing' it with design elements that imply a comfortable rural lifestyle."

Since Fogo de Chao means "fire in the earth" or "chimney," for his opening design statement Cooper showcases the glassed-in, flaming rotisseries set in a limestone base up front at the entrance and viewable from the street. This element is topped with color graduated ceramic tiles on the façade that suggest flames below and the sky above. Thus, from the street the rotisserie gets full exposure and the corner entrance resembles a rising chimney.

The bar/waiting area in the entry, provides a "comfortable low key" area apart from the bustling activity of the dining rooms. The use of granite, polished woods and slab glass ties this area in with the dining rooms that follow. Central to the dining experience and the main dining room is the salad bar. Opposite the lavish display of salad selections is an equally spectacular, wrap around wine-room which combines storage with display. Guests are exposed to both these featured attractions as they are led to their tables in either of the two dining rooms. There is a third room—for private functions.

A dramatic and lively element in the main dining room is the 40 ft. long "waterfall wall" of stylized timbers that alludes to the Brazilian rainforest. The dining room "looks polished, yet natural" with its slate flooring, wrought iron and burnished wood partitions, and the hand cast stained glass and metal chandeliers. Over much of the ceiling is an arrangement of louvered panels that tends to bring the outdoors indoors as they also filter the lights set behind the panels.

The private dining room features a 35 ft. mural showing the traditions and lifestyles of the gauchos of the Rio Grande de Sol region. Glass and stone walls, stained glass chandeliers and stacked cordwood near a roaring fireplace "reflect the naturalness and civility of the region."

MOJITO

ST. LOUIS PARK, MN

DESIGN — *Shea Architects, Minneapolis, MN*
David A. Shea: Creative Director & Principal
Steve Haasl: Architect & Principal
Gerry Ewald: Interior Designer

PHOTOGRAPHY — *Farri & Forrai Photographers*

In Mojito, the flavor-full restaurant in St. Louis Park, the South American influences exude from the ambiance created by Shea Architects as well as from the meaty dishes. The client wanted a restaurant where the emphasis is on theatrical cooking in a relaxed, laid-back environment and the Shea design team created a design that conveys the desired "mood and personality."

The decor is urban yet comfortable with lofty ceilings and soft greenery accents throughout. Dark woods complement the caramel-cream colored walls and the sharp, bright colored accents abound: crisp greens, earthy reds and cool blues. The bar, shaped like a question mark, starts at the lounge level and steps down to a lower level. On the raised lounge level, patrons at the bar sit at regulation height chairs while higher stools are needed at the light marble surfaced bar at the lower level. A rich, forest green back bar wall sets the scene for 12 backlit photo boxes. Wines and liquor bottles are stored at either end. The green upholstered pillows in the lounge are set against a dramatically illuminated wall paved with rough stones.

The display kitchen glistens in stainless steel while screens, dividers and decorative black wrought iron units recall the Hispanic heritage of the restaurant's cuisine. In the giant rotisserie, meat, game and poultry are skewered and roasted. Sweeping curves in the ceiling patterns follow through on the floor and in the placement of the vibrant green upholstered booths that caress the arced partitions.

Freestanding tables fill in the open areas. In a semi-private dining room—a high backed banquette curves along the partition with tables angled to follow the sweep of the line. Along the fabric draped window wall other tables are lined up. The custom fixtures and finishes throughout all of Mojito make the design unique and memorable for the diners.

BLUE

CHARLOTTE, NC

DESIGN — *Little Diversified Architectural Consulting,
Charlotte, NC*
Steve Starr: Studio Principal

PHOTOGRAPHY — *Peter Brentlinger*

The 8500 sq. ft. "talk of the town" restaurant/bar/lounge in
Charlotte, NC is Blue. As designed by Little, "Blue captures
your senses and triggers your curiosity." The visitor enters
into a vast space and, according to the designers, "swims in a
sea of Mediterranean, multi-culture cuisine."

What the designers hoped to accomplish, as shown in these photos, was "to abstractly contrast land and sea." The design team emphasized the solidity and order of the existing structural columns (the land) while complementing these with soft, flowing curves (the sea). The result is four distinct dining spaces including a "modish" bar area. The bar is anchored by a curved bar and a circular inset floor of mosaic tiles in a dark timber surround. More circles sweep overhead and continue the floor inset motif. Guests can gather here for a drink or they may dine here as well. The space is designed as the major focal element in Blue with a circular stage and well planned acoustics to accommodate live performances. "The bar exudes energy and style while maintaining a sense of scale so dining guests are not disturbed."

The bi-level dining area affords a view of the stage in the bar. Here soft greens dominate on the upholstery, carpeting and wall treatments. The green is complemented by big blasts of rich marine blue from panels over the banquettes along the straight perimeter wall. Square acoustic panels hang down from the blacked out ceiling and these red panels are softly illuminated.

The restaurant/bar has received a 4-star rating and is the most popular of Charlotte's new "in" places.

ZAYTINYA

DESIGN — *Adamstein & Demetriou Architects, Washington, DC*
Olvia Demetriouu, FAIS / Theo Adamstein —
Principals & Designers
Bernard Holnaider — Project Manager
Stacey West — Interior Designer
Griz Dwight — AIA

PHOTOGRAPHY — *Maxwell MacKenzie*

"Our client requested that the design capture the qualities of the Mediterranean and its architecture, specifically the dramatic, volcanic island of Santorini. They wanted the design to be contemporary, with a high energy feel reflecting the well priced menu. They required high volume seating, flexibility for large groups and the interior had to be casual yet sophisticated." Olvia Demetriou and Theo Adamstein, the principals/designers of Zaytinya in Washington, DC had to satisfy these requirements for a restaurant that would feature

Eastern Mediterranean cuisine: Greek, Turkish and Lebanese—but creatively reinterpreted.

The source of inspiration for the design was the organic quality of the whitewashed architecture of Santorini and the palette ranging from pure white to every shade of blue. "Using a language of 'visual collage'," we brought together elements, interior gestures, forms and finishes that evoke the feeling of the region—without specific literal references." The dominant element in the larger dining room is the sweeping vaulted ceiling. It provides a soft transition from the 24 ft. ceiling to the areas where the ceiling is only ten ft. Four distinct and separate levels help "to create a sense of the terracing and height one finds in Santorini." Accentuating the curve of the vault is the massive, two story marble grid that holds large white candles. This unit also serves as a screen for the raised bar area and it opens up towards the entrance.

The two ends of the restaurant are distinguished by fireplaces. One is carved out of the mezzanine wall while the other—a slab of white marble—leans against the navy blue

wall. "The fireplaces give a special quality to these dining areas, making them more intimate and cozy." Throughout the space white, ice blue, periwinkle and navy blue come together to define areas. Where the ceilings are lowest "we used saturated color to give these areas a unique quality." The whitewashed, textured walls, finished concrete and dark timber floors, the wood millwork, white marble and satin and blackened steel are softened by the vinyl, faux suede, woven velvets and linen textured fabrics in shades of periwinkle used for upholstery and pillows.

Zaytinya can seat 200 in the dining areas, 42 at the bar and an additional 90 on the outdoor patio.

TIZI MELLOUL

CHICAGO, IL

DESIGN — *Suhail Design Studio, Chicago, IL*
Suhail: Designer/Principal

PHOTOGRAPHY — *Doug Fogelson*

For Suhail, the Chicago-based designer, the challenge in designing this 2700 sq. ft. space on N. Wells in Chicago was "to combine two existing spaces into one cohesive experience"—while infusing Tizi Melloul restaurant/lounge with the ambiance and flavor of Morocco.

"Having traveled throughout Morocco, I was able to record certain experiences I felt should somehow resonate within the concept," said Suhail. "Everything from sunsets over the whitewashed rooftops of Casablanca to the aromatic spice markets, the colors and sounds of the souks

(native markets)—to the whirling dervishes—I wanted the Moroccan components to be authentic." To assure their authenticity, Suhail worked with Moroccan merchants and artisans who provided the furniture, lighting fixtures and artwork. The result is not an exact copy of "an old world Moroccan café" but an experience that captures "elements of Moroccan visual intensity interpreted with post modern flair."

The sinuous, curving space is divided into five zones. There are two major dining areas and a bar/lounge. A foyer leads into the lounge that in turn opens to the dining areas. A sleek, elliptical bar is off to one side of the lounge that has textured, creamy white plastered walls and custom ceiling light fixtures that suggest the tops of nomadic tents. The floor-recessed lighting adds to the Casablanca atmosphere and enhances the details on the Moroccan chairs, tables and pouf-ottomans that furnish this space.

The Crown Room can seat 65 guests. This is a fiery blast of typically Moroccan red, burgundy, lilac and brown. The colors are combined to "evoke the earth intensity of Marakesh." The crown refers to the King of Morocco. While the chairs and tables are ultra modern Italian designs, the wall hangings and lamps are pure Moroccan as are the copper topped tables designed by Suhail. To achieve the contemporary/traditional look, the designer combined wood, fiberglass, foam and copper in this space. Typically Moroccan is the use of mosaic tiles which here appear on the soffit to enhance rather than detract from the total composition.

The Crescent Room is the more "traditional" dining area and it is blue: blue walls, blue wall hangings, and a blue crescent moon—another Moroccan symbol. This is the communal dining room and guests are invited to eat with their fingers as they semi-recline or sit on low semicircular banquettes that caress the wall. The atmosphere here is of the interior of a Bedouin tent.

Two other dining areas—to make up the five zones (like the five points of the Moroccan star) are to be added. "The final aesthetic is a fusion of traditional and contemporary concepts and what I felt a space in Chicago should feel and look like if it were to represent Morocco in some way."

TANTRA

LOS ANGELES, CA

DESIGN — *Akar Studios, Los Angeles, CA*
Sat Garg, AIA: Principal
Kristi Jack / Claire Downes: Designers

MURAL — *Sat Garg; Executed by Alex & Kirsty Campbell*

PHOTOGRAPHY — *Randall Michelson*

Tantra, the brilliant and captivating restaurant on Sunset Blvd. in the Silver Lake area of Los Angeles, is the shared dream of father and son, Navri and R.J. Singh. This is their concept of Indian dining and to set the culinary tone as

"high class," Singh wanted Michelin star chef Vineet Bhatia to oversee the menu development. For a colorful, playful, sexy and still relaxed ambiance in which to enjoy the culinary experience, the owners called upon Sat Garg of Akar Studios of Los Angeles for the interior design.

"From the moment a guest enters Tantra, an atmosphere rich in Indian style and hospitality welcomes." The space is lush and sensual and filled with India-inspired hues and textures. Saffron yellow, cinnamon red and earthy wheat are highlighted with fuchsia, lemon yellow and sky blue. The name "Tantra" is from a Sanskrit scripture that deals with practices between a man and a woman—both meditative and sexual—to attain god. To start the Tantra journey, Sat Garg created his depiction of "tantric energy emanating between a gender fusion of man and woman." This vision is repeated on a smaller scale in the lounge. "Hammered copper doors, dramatic iron sand silk light fixtures, fabric-canopied dining nooks and a curtain of oxidized metal dangling over a narrow water shelf are a few of the highlights that create this Indian fantasy scene."

While a DJ spins eclectic music, the large, cinnamon-red colored lounge area accommodates 100 guests who can enjoy exotic cocktails or regular bar drinks. Since the lounge has a separate entrance it can be closed off to cater to private parties. The lounge is usually inhabited by "cool but relaxed" local artists, writers, musicians and actors who "embrace

eclectic, ethnic cuisine." From the entry, guests move past mottled, deep yellow plaster walls to get to the earthen wheat colored dining room.

Lord Ganesha, the God of Prosperity, watches over and blesses the 75 guests who can be seated here. Along the walls there is banquette seating while smaller, freestanding tables are in the center. For special private parties of up to 12 guests there is a large, silk-canopied area in the room. The designers' inspiration came from the colorful character of urban streets and villas of Western India. Sat Garg has infused the 7300 sq. ft. space with an outdoor feeling by "using color as a fuse and common denominator. Rich mottled tones emit a sense of warmth and sensuality and reflect the canvas of India's ever changing background." All the furniture, furnishings, lamp shades, graphics and lighting were custom designed by Akar Studios for Tantra.

SEA

BROOKLYN, NY

DESIGN — *Charoonkit Thahong*
Teeraya Meesupaya: Assistant

LIGHTING CONSULTANT — *Chotima*
Photjananuwat

PHOTOGRAPHY — *Udom*

The 7500 sq. ft., street level space that is S.E.A, is located on N. 6th St. in Brooklyn. The Thai restaurant/lounge was designed by Charoonkit Thahong and his client requested that the design include a Buddha and "real cool bathrooms." From there on—anything goes—so long as it stays within a tight budget. The concept was to create "an urban destination that was casually hip—like the neighborhood."

First and foremost Kit Thahong had to divide the wide space into dining and bar areas. Then, using light—a very important element in shaping the spaces—colored the areas and created the desired moods. Kit then further divided the areas with light: internally lit wood panels, sheer fabric draperies and various kinds of furniture—all "to create a warm and cozy space." Two new skylights were opened in the ceiling and new beams were added to support them. "Overall the structure remains the same—but clean, painted and polished."

The focal point of the entire space is the reflecting pool and the Budda sitting beside it. The statue is backed by a lotus screen. In the bar/lounge area it is the mirrored ball that adds a sense of sparkle and retro, 70s fun. The materials used throughout were simple and unassuming: plywood, raw cement, metal and some frosted glass. The communal tables, benches, stools and coffee tables were fashioned of wood salvaged from the site and most surfaces were covered with clear urethane "to reveal their own material color." The dining tables were painted black as were some of the wood divider panels.

As mentioned, Sea is divided by colored light that permeates and tints everything around it. The front area and the 70s inspired bar glows red; the swinging benches, a hanging bubble chair and even diner-like, dish lighting fixtures. A second bar is washed in a yellow/gold light. It is here in the center of the space that Buddha sits contemplating the underwater spotlights in the pool that is suggestive of the floating markets of Thailand.

A green light suffuses the dining room in between. To enter the bathrooms is like going to hell! It is blazing red and a spy monitor in the cylindrical toilets circulates images taken of the dining room, the bar, and the street outside." The hip clients think it is "real cool."

MIE N YU

WASHINGTON, DC

DESIGN — *Core Architecture + Design, Washington, DC
and EROC Builders Peter F. Hapstak lll, AIA, IIDA, ISP
Dale Stewart, AIA / Bo Soon Kim / Brian Calis / Brian
Miller / Jeffrey Deffenbaugh / Jiyun Park / Kathleen Clare
Ngiam / Kevin Coyne / Tomas Quijano*

PHOTOGRAPHY — *Michael Moran Photography,
New York, NY*

"A new type of eating and drinking experience—more satisfying than a bar, less formal than a restaurant, and increasingly preferred by diners of all ages and means." This is how a magazine described the "boutique nightery," Mie N Yu.

The historic 1909 Georgetown façade tells you something about what is about to happen but what counts is the magic that occurs when the guest enters. The theme is Asian but it is never made clear or distinct which region or country of that vast continent is featured. "We wanted to recreate the atmosphere of a busy street bazaar; we built structures to house seating groups and made small intimate areas in what would otherwise be a large open space." The guests pass by a pair of Monk sentinels stationed near "sublime fountains and then welcomed into a garden-like setting." The Chinese-influenced English standing bar "radiates a feeling of old Hong Kong." Setting the mood for the lounging and dining is the DJ's area which is actually a part of the back bar. The booth looms out over the bar patrons and an elevated Turkish tent beyond—with its ornate ottomans and cozy daybeds—"beckons diners to set a spell." Tiled fountains, a gigantic, hand-forged bird cage and "architectural relics that

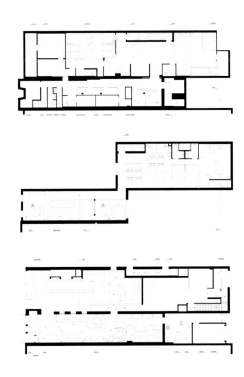

create intimate elevated dining nooks lined in silk and brocade" appear in the Moroccan "street bazaar" setting.

The Venetian Bar, on the mezzanine, invites communal diners to "mingle among the mirrored, candle-lit walls." This leads to a formal dining room. Here the red velvet draped walls surround the mirrored tables set beneath, reflecting prism chandeliers. Rustic high chairs made from old teak-wood fencing pull up to these tables. For special entertaining there is the Dragon Lounge that has its own "discreet private entrance" and its own DJ.

SUSHI SAMBA

CHICAGO, IL

DESIGN — *The Rockwell Group, New York, NY*
David Rockwell

CLIENTS — *Shimon Bokooza / Danielle Billera /*
Mathew Johnson

PHOTOGRAPHY — *Mark Ballogg,*
Steinkamp Ballogg Photography.

What could be more yin-yang—more of an "odd couple" than a marriage of Brazilian and Japanese cultures—and their cuisines—and still have it register as a unique and memorable "brand" all of its own? Well, the answer to the above, as illustrated here, lies in the design solution and the design talents of David Rockwell and The Rockwell Group of New York. The 9000 sq. ft. space in what was previously

the Hudson Club in Chicago now throbs to a beat all of its own and features a bar/lounge area that can accommodate almost 80 guests and a main dining room that seats 140 and 20 more at the sushi bar. There is also a private room for parties of up to 80 guests.

According to the design team, "We are combining the cultures in a multitude of ways: color and texture, warms and cools, yin and yang." It starts on the façade where uniquely shaped awnings convex and concave from the building and the entrance and street side windows are Mondrian patterned with panels of clear and colored glass. Reds, blues, yellows and golds—in various materials and textures—appear throughout the space and carry through the feeling of water and fire.

Curtains of steel beads appear as dividers, partitions or hang from the ceiling to create a focal area above the recessed seating in the center of the dining room in the "water-fire pit." The bar/lounge is up front, and golden "waterfall" panels of beads separate the "fiery" seating in the lounge. The bar seems to float in a pool of blue light and multi-blue tones of mosaic tiles pave the back bar. Amber plastic shelves are suspended in air off the back bar. Throughout the space, amber/gold glass shades cast a warm glow over the scene.

The entire restaurant is on the first floor and the space is distinguished by the curving yellow/gold walls that rise up from behind the deep red colored booths and soar as they angle forward to reach the blacked out ceiling. The sushi bar serves food and "viewing entertainment" in the center of the space under a canopy of blue-tinted strings of beads. Hanging from the ceiling are unusual, convoluted, boat-shaped light fixtures while simpler drum-shaped shades hang over the "U"-shaped booths along the perimeter wall. There is a private dining room in the rear with a Mojito bar and it is closed off from the main dining room by a Mondrian wall comprised of fabrics and glass. At the mezzanine level there is a DJ as well as lounge seating. The bathrooms with their frosted glass walls is a "must go—must see" attraction at Sushi Samba. Like most of the Rockwell Group projects, the colored theatrical effects make the place even more vital and exciting.

The meat packing district of New York City is not only gentrifying but it is rapidly becoming a major location for top fashion designers and "unique experience dining" establishments. Meet, on Gansevoort St., is one of the latter and as designed by Adam Kushner of Kushner Studios working with Master Tin Sun, a Feng Shui specialist, it is something different. The former "meat freezer" has been "transformed into a contemporary restaurant emphasizing luxury and comfort unbridled by pretension. The name "Meet" is a play on "words and worlds" and is a unique blend of sensuous atmosphere, sleek modern design and the touch of Feng Shui."

"Seen through the French windows and kissed by the glow of backlit mirrors, patrons seated in the dining area's low-backed banquettes appear to be floating in glass." A luminous, arced catwalk runs dramatically from the entrance all the way to the rear of the space and the upward slope—alongside the bar—"the catwalk builds upon a voyeuristic concept via a play on notions of perspective." The catwalk's incline allows patrons at one end of the bar to stand waist high while at the other end imbibers are chest high at the

MEET

NEW YORK, NY

ARCHITECT/DESIGN — *Kushner Studios, New York, NY*

GRAPHIC DESIGN — *Victoria O'Young*

FENG SHUI CONSULTANT — *Master Tin Sun*

PHOTOGRAPHY — *Seth Boyd, New York, NY*

bar that is topped with a slab of glowing amber onyx. A
lounge area on the left is sunken and furnished with floating, ultra-suede banquettes and ostrich leather seating in
taupes and browns. In addition to booths along the rear wall
and the two intimate alcoves, there is a raised Chef's table
that serves as a focal point in the dining room. Angled mirrors on the walls "afford interplay with the rest of the space."
The panels of the alcoves are finished with two-toned
coconut wood as is the floor of the catwalk.

In Meet's Café, the Emperor-style chairs are crafted
from woven rattan and the tabletops are composed of finished coconut wood. "To ensure an harmonious flow of
energies," Feng Shui specialist Master Tin Sun was consult-
ed on the layout of the space, materials, colors and the
placement of objects. All these complement the "relaxed
chic" Mediterranean-inspired cuisine of Executive Chef,
Ten L. Vong.

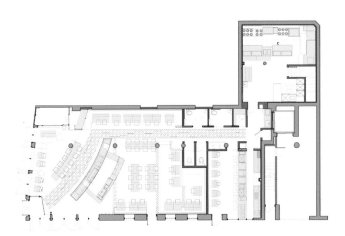

THE GINGER MAN

NEW YORK, NY

DESIGN — *Tree House Design Ltd., New York, NY*
Julius S. "Jack" Baum

PHOTOGRAPHY — *Stephan J. Carr Photography, NY*

The Ginger Man is a beer bar that recently opened in the Murray Hill section of Manhattan. The name is derived from a book of the same name that chronicled the life of an American expatriate living in Dublin and enjoying "the good life," usually with very little money. The owner of the bar wanted to create a place for people like the hero of that book (Sebastian Dangerfield) "with a clear love of beer and a place where like-minded folk could gather to drink and converse."

A selection of 66 imported beers on draft and over 100 high quality imported bottle brews plus prime single malt

scotches are available in the 3000 sq. ft. "almost historic environment." As designed by Jack Baum of Tree House Design, the space feels as if it were over a century old even though it is new and built from scratch. "It is set in Ireland and the space had to convey that sense of affection for pubs and a reverence to alcohol that is unique to that country." It all starts with the cast iron storefront and the leaded textured antique glass that reinforces the effect.

The 45 ft. long bar with the polished copper back bar and the 66 beer taps set into it sets the scene. Above the taps are displayed glass drinking flasks and a ledge filled with hard-to-find, beer glasses provided by obscure beer producers from around the world. Back bar chalk boards and illumi-

nated vitrines also recall the Irish Pub connection. Copper lamps with mica shades stand atop the bar to cast a glow over the polished, dark-stained oak bar. Opposite the bar is a massive, 15 ft. long, solid oak table with a 6 in. slab top that is sturdy enough—should the "spirits" move one—to dance upon. The Jacobean design table is flanked and surrounded by 8 ft. oak paneling with concealed lights on top. Designed into the wainscoting are antique beveled mirror panels and period sconces with hand-blown glass shades. At each side of the table are built-in banquettes.

The floor is laid with oak planks "which have been left to deteriorate under the daily siege of patrons and splattered beer." The main room has a 15 ft. high, coffered ceiling and from it hang five antique bronze chandeliers retrofitted to accommodate reproduction Edison light bulbs. The ceiling is lower at the rear of the bar and the pressed tin here has

the patina of copper and terra cotta "with a look of a tobacco glaze from 100 years of cigar smoke." In this carpeted space with upholstered furniture, floor lamps and wall sconces, one feels as though one were in a run-down parlour of an Irish estate. On the walls is an anaglyptic wallcovering and the illuminated vitrines are filled with more drinking memorabilia.

Hand painted on the rear wall is the owner's philosophy. It is a quote from the book: "When you don't have any money, the problem is food. When you have money, it's sex. When you have both, it's health. If everything is simply Jake—then you're frightened to death."

COMERCIAL

DESIGN — *Stadler + Partner, Munich, Germany*
Stuart Stadler / Michael Onischke

PHOTOGRAPHY — *Andreas Pohlmann*

Located in a new business center in Munich, Germany is Comercial, a bar designed by Stadler + Partner of the same city. The "Italian" styled bar can seat 60 inside but accommodate another 80 standing guests as well. Weather permitting, 45 guests can enjoy their drinks or light repasts out of doors. In addition to wine and cocktail service, patrons can get small warm meals and coffee. There are two entrances into Comercial: one from the business building and the other off the street. The ground plan was determined by the kitchen rectangle that cuts into the bar area and thus formed the L-shaped bar which is almost 55 ft. long. Another factor in the space design was the staircase that leads to the basement.

The high tech industrial look of Comercial starts with the open ceiling soaring overhead and roughly textured with fire retardant material. In contrast is the solid oak and stainless steel bar that starts parallel to the all-glass façade on the street side entrance and then makes a right turn to accommodate the kitchen. The kitchen is visible through an opening in a wall covered with diamond shaped mirrors. The balance of the walls are covered with a custom fabric with a red and beige damask/floral pattern. Opposite the bar, the walls go up part way and are tuft upholstered in brown. The same material is used as a canopy that cantilevers out over the benches, stools and tables lined up along the tufted wall. Highlighting and creating distinct seating groups are the red/orange shaded lamps that extend out from circular cut-outs where the tufted panels meet. Lighting is recessed into the canopy as well.

A long metal trough runs over the bar and it lights up the bar area. All the lights can be dimmed "so the atmosphere can be changed and the lighting can be adapted for daytime and nighttime."

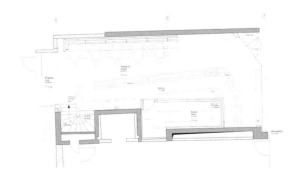

In keeping with the elegant and sophisticated design of The Bellagio Hotel Casino in Las Vegas and in contrast to the Vegas Strip which is vibrant with color, lights and noise, the Nectar Bar as designed by Jordan Mozer is all cool and elegant. The Nectar Bar serves as "a liquid-cool, high energy liquor bar/raw bar" at the end of one of the Hotel's entry axis. The entrances into the bar are sculptured, irregular-shaped arches that introduce the amorphous look of the bar.

Filled with soft, sinuous and serpentine lines that are almost a Mozer signature, the bar itself undulates across the space. Its snaky movement is echoed by the stainless steel foot rail and the row of body-hugging, organic stools of white steel. The walls are sculpted plaster and the seamless, almost white terrazzo floor curves up and becomes the base of the bar. Cast magnesium/aluminum alloy and stainless steel provide the metallic bar tops and other metal accents in the space.

A bulbous column emanates from the center of the space—similar to the other elements in the design—and reaches up to an oddly formed dome that encompasses most of Nectar Bar, like a mushroom cap atop a mushroom stem. Liquor is displayed in soft shadow boxes along the wall

NECTAR

LAS VEGAS, NV

DESIGN — *Jordan Mozer Associates, Chicago, IL Jordan Mozer: Principal/Designer*

PHOTOGRAPHY — *Doug Snower, Doug Snower Photography*

backed up with backlit panels of assorted colored glass. In
addition to seating at the bar there are freestanding tables
with polished glass mosaic tops on stainless steel bases. Taller
tables—also poised on stainless steel bases—are clustered to
one side of the central column and they are serviced by
sculpted mono-pod metal stools.

Lighting is subtly introduced at the base of the dome,
under the lip of the bar, behind the wall shadow boxes, from
blown and poured art glass lamps, and the recessed mini
spots that ring the dome in the ceiling.

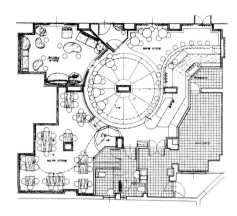

Taking its name Nazca from the high Peruvian planes, the designers at Studio Ciccotti of Rome created this fun bar/lounge/café in the historic area of old Rome. "We made unusual architectonic choices, both in the use of materials and in the design and tone of the furnishings—trying to adapt new materials to ancient uses and using traditional materials in new ways." The space has been conceived as a "sinuous cavern" with a central well under a blue sky visible through an overhead opening. The "rocks" are mounted in steps like the natural stratification of stone while a blue disk illuminated by fiber optics represents the sky.

The bar is centrally located (the well) and is visible from throughout Nazca. "The fluid plane and the red light

NAZCA

ROME, ITALY

DESIGN — *Studio Ciccotti, Rome, Italy*

PHOTOGRAPHY — *Courtesy of Studio Ciccotti*

of the rear counter seem to echo a terrestrial Magna." The high ceiling room is fitted with rough hewn wood, and acidified steel is used to simulate iron on the counters, seats, and the central dish and bottle carrier which has been laser etched with ethnic symbols. Large smoked mirrors with "translucent veils draped over them" seem to visibly enlarge the space and "give the effect of the absence of time limits."

In the private areas the low tables are covered with shattered glass. Drum shaped poufs are used for seating. The central column is covered with mosaics.

"The gilt wall pictures and other touches harmoniously complement the place and render it full and rich with atmosphere."

GLASS

DESIGN — *Leeser Architecture, Brooklyn, NY*
Thomas Leeser

PHOTOGRAPHER — *Mathu Placek*

A bright, light and glowing ambiance is emitted from Glass—an oasis of excitement on Tenth Ave. in the Chelsea area of Manhattan where it exists amid old garages and dilapidated storefronts. A full height sheet of blue glass in the façade simultaneously serves as part of the façade design and as the backing for the mirror of the unisex bathroom that is located up front in Glass and can be seen from the street. Guests washing their hands at the his/hers trough-like sink are in full view behind the illuminated blue glass panel.

As designed by Thomas Leeser of Leeser Architecture, the space behind the bathrooms is like the hull of an airplane—curved and compact. The digitally-generated space suggests the fluidity of virtual environments, Seats bend out

of the surface of the wall and extend floating in the room."
In another sweep of curves and arcs, the bar is "literally the
floor curving up and back towards the customers." Shelves
emerge out of the translucent wall panels behind the bar to
hold the liquor display. Throughout, there is a seamless flowing together of walls, ceilings and bar front.

The wall opposite the bar consists of high, swooped
back banquettes covered in assorted blue upholstery fabrics.
In front of the wall seating are white topped tables and
white, crushed-in ball-like plastic seats set out on the mini-
tiled floor. A small enclosed courtyard can be viewed
through the rear glass wall. The only view is upward towards
the sky and the neighboring industrial buildings. Pink, red
and blue argon light emit from the edges of the new structure "tinting the interior in what are the only colors
around." Inside Leeser are fitted halogen lamps flush with
the ceiling and five ft. apart: five over the banquette seating
area and three over the bar.

According to the designer, "The design is inspired and
reminiscent of the interior of a luxury car, while at the
same time it is rather sparse, minimal and monochromatic—more like the functional, minimal aesthetic of a racing
car." According to the hip, young crowd that frequent
Glass—it's cool!!

GHOSTBAR

LAS VEGAS, NV

DESIGN CONCEPT — *Scott De Graff, Michael Morton: owners and 555 Design Fabrication & Management*

DESIGN — *555 Design Fabrication & Management, Chicago, IL*
James Geier

PHOTOGRAPHY — *Nine Group LLC*

Way up on the top floor of the new Palms Casino & Resort on W. Flamingo Rd. in Las Vegas is the GhostBar and Lounge. Reached by a private elevator and heralded in the entrance lobby with a 13 ft. neon and stainless Ghost logo, the rooftop bar and lounge affords a spectacular view of the color and light filled Vegas strip. The interior space as designed by James Geier and the design team at 555—working closely with the owners Scott De Graff and Michael

Morton—is filled with high tech, metallic silver, acid green and rich blues that all seem to sparkle and shimmer. Lights reflect and play upon the glass mosaic-covered piers that frame the 14 ft. tall windows and the unhindered view of Vegas from this aerie location. Cut out of the ceiling is a 30 ft. long Ghost logo that is neon lit and programmed to change color moods and intensity as the night progresses and it pulsates with the music provided by the resident DJ. The front of the long bar is finished with undulating woven stainless fabric which has been dyed a metallic blue and is further enhanced by back lighting. From the backlit back bar an eerie and ghost-ly glow is cast and the bottles are displayed on stainless shelves that float across the panels. Patrons can relax on custom, ultra contemporary furniture designed for lounging while enjoying the music, the action and the views.

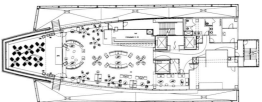

In addition to the main lounge that can seat 150 or accommodate 300 at a reception, there is a VIP lounge for 20 "high rollers" finished in silver and lime. The deck beyond the expanse of glass can entertain another 75 guests. Here there is a 360 degree panoramic view with posh seating areas enhanced with fiber optically lit drink rails that run around most of the deck's circumference. A glass inset in the flooring—near the rail—offers a "jaw-dropping view" straight down to the street.

Tied in with the adjacent disco is the Opera Bar located in the Larcomar Entertainment Center in Lima, Peru. "We designed the space to have a 'blue feeling'—to serve as a transition to the disco," said Jose Orrego of Metropolis, the designer of the bar. The shimmering entrance façade is made up of shattered glass and that gives way to a fractured view of the deep blue, dark interior. Inside, the floors are blends of cement, nogal wood and high-tech, industrial stamped metal sheets around the curved bar which is faced with assorted shades and tints of gray mosaic tile. The bar is located in the center of the 110 sq. meter space and the sweeping lines of the bar, the round columns and the arcs of metal railing all add to a sense of rhythm and sensuality of Opera Bar. Adding to that feeling is the blue light emanating from the hidden neon strips under the curved ceiling elements, and the black light and the down lights that reflect off the blue painted surfaces. One feature wall is highlighted with a harlequin design executed in three shades of blue.

Nogal wood frames the windows that have a view out to the water while wood frames also outline an open viewing area into the disco next door. This frame is equipped with a "retro black light" that illuminates the blue wall around it. "The mood is blue—and fashionable," says Orrego.

OPERA BAR

LIMA, PERU

DESIGN — *Metropolis, Lima, Peru, Jose Orrego*

PHOTOGRAPHY — *Jose Orrego*

TURF LOUNGE

TORONTO, ON

DESIGN — *Hirschberg Design Group, Toronto, ON*
Martin Hirschberg: Principal

PHOTOGRAPHY — *Joy Von Tiedemann, Toronto, ON*

"Woodline Entertainment wanted to change the direction of horse racing and make it more entertaining and accessible to a new, tech savvy generation of urban professionals." To accomplish this, Martin Hirschberg and the Hirschberg Design Group of Toronto, created the Turf Lounge. The 8000 sq. ft. space is divided into four distinct areas: bar, smoking room, dining room and gaming room. Each has its own distinct character and ambiance. Located in the heart of the financial district of Toronto, the design blends historic architecture and modern design "to create a conservative yet contemporary space."

The bar is located beyond the foyer—past the overhead

floating canopy and the contemporary geometric overtones in a palette of rich browns. Historic arched windows and limestone walls surround the expansive, ebony finished bar. A four story bronze mesh curtain accentuates the height of this space that a century ago was a bank. Above the internally-lit back bar is a frieze of TV monitors showing sporting events and there is even a stock market ticker running above the running horses.

In the dining room, the custom made tables and wing back chairs "evoke a traditional drawing room feel" while the tall tan booths on the short wall with their own LCD television and network jacks for internet access provide "the latest in modern advancements." The other bettors are kept up to the minute via the flat screen TV monitors on the surrounding walls. "In all the rooms, Turf Lounge is a geometric study of positive and negative space, plane and volume, scale and proportion, lightness and darkness. The rich brown tone palette creates an environment in which old and new are simultaneously contrasted and integrated."

GALAXY BAR/LOUNGE

SHANGHAI, CHINA

DESIGN — *Joseph Wong Design Associates (JWDA),*
San Diego, CA
Joseph Wong: Principal/Designer

PHOTOGRAPHY — *JWDA*

By winning an international design competition, Joseph Wong Design Associates of San Diego was commissioned to design and coordinate the renovation and remodeling of the Galaxy Hotel in Shanghai, China. This hotel is the "most prized and special property" held by Jin Jiang International Hotel Management Group.

"The first floor lobby was initially composed of spaces that did not connect." The existing escalator, which was too

"mall-like," was replaced by a glass staircase and the designers took advantage of the open space to reposition the Bar and Lounge and include a discreet and intimate gourmet restaurant as well as a hotel canteen. The new space of the lounge has been expanded into what was a small portion of the exterior garden and includes a new glass wall "that gives those relaxing in its environs a sense of harmony and security."

The original white marble floors remain but the look of the bar/lounge is softened by an undulating stripe pattern carpet in cream and apricot that swirls diagonally across the space. Palm trees, growing up through the marble floor, truly turn this open and gracious area into an oasis with the elliptical bar as the featured attraction. The stone clad bar encompasses a silvery round column that supports the mezzanine under which the bar is set. The tiered silvery bar displays liquor bottles on two levels.

"Further design details that add to the munificent ambiance are the varied stonework, the precise details such as the tiled ceilings and the charming artificial stream that runs through the lobby with its artificial glass lily pads that guide the eye through the playful, but discreet space"—to the bar and the comfortable, pale colored chairs of the lounge.

PIANO BAR

ST. JULIAN, MALTA

DESIGN — *Di Leonardo International, Warwick, RI*

PHOTOGRAPHY — *Warren Jagger*

In creating the Piano Bar and other public spaces in the Hotel Intercontinental Malta, in the St. Julian area of the island, the designers of Di Leonardo International carried forth a contemporary design style reminiscent of sleek ocean liners. "This was inspired by the creative architectural solution demanded by the site and produced by the architect and engineers." Working within the dramatic spaces, the interior designers were able "to create interesting view corridors and features throughout the space."

The sectional relationship is evident in the stepped level Piano Bar and the interior gardens that are experienced at different elevations. "This adds a dramatic and unexpected twist to an evening at the bar." The lobby lounge flanks the main lobby and sheer curtains line the tall windows that make up part of the bar/lounge space. Other walls and the curved bar itself are clad in a light colored natural wood which is complemented by the light wood floor border and the handsome darker wood of the upholstered bar stools.

Camel back loveseats and sofas covered in a deep burgundy fabric serve as the nuclei for the individual clusters of seating around low, glass-topped, cocktail tables with rocker-like bases. The high backed, tuft upholstered pull up chairs are upholstered in saffron gold leather and the combination of the red and gold with daubs of blue on the speckled carpet unifies the space.

The sophisticated lighting system in the lounge makes it possible to create different atmospheres for different times of the day. "The changing of the wood tones for the holding lounge to the main restaurant enabled the lounge to be highly active during the day when the restaurant is closed." At night—the spaces tend to blend. "The furnishings are sophisticated and contemporary and are a unique contrast to the work by local artists."

FLOW BAR

DENVER, CO

DESIGN — *Semple Brown Design, Denver, CO*

PHOTOGRAPHY — *Ron Pollard*

Clean lines, contemporary designer furniture and subtle lighting distinguish the Flow Bar as designed by Semple Brown of Denver. The Luna Hotel, in the LoDo historic district of Denver, is home to the lively bar to the left of the entrance and a café to the right. They are set there "to engage guests immediately and welcome them" as they make their way to the registration desk in the rear. Flow Bar was designed to have an urban feel but with warm, hip elements.

Semple Brown's team opened up the space. They wanted "to create a completely different concept for the space— something that was more open and inviting to not only the hotel guests but to restaurant and bar patrons as well."

The new design includes the Velocity Coffee & Crepes Café off the lobby as well as the lounge and the intimate Elexer Bar. One level up, accessed by the wide and gracious

stairway with soft lighting, a glass fronted bar and inviting upscale seating, "the Flow Bar is a perfect place to meet and mingle." Keeping the energy and atmosphere alive and exciting are the changing colors that fade and grow and transform into new colors behind the tall glass bar and under the bar seating. The Flow Bar flows. The lounge is located above the lower lobby and the stairwell. Its clear and open design provides a "sneak peek" to the action below. In the lounge, seating is provided in public or private booths and, like the rest of the bar/lounge, they are illuminated by soft candle-light.

A full service kitchen serves appetizers and room service while the Elexer Bar, at the lobby lounge level, creates a more subtle and intimate setting than the Flow Bar upstairs.

CHURCH LOUNGE

NEW YORK, NY

DESIGN — *Bogdanow Partners Architects, New York, NY*
Larry Bogdanow / Warren Ashworth / Tom Schweitzer /
Randi Halpern / Brian Slocum

PHOTOGRAPHY — *Tsao & McKown*

Chambers, a separate, club-like room, adjoins the Church Lounge and is available for private functions. It is furnished with widely-spaced, Victorian-style seating poufs segmented into six sections with decorative cord, and finished with deep fringes. Subtle lighting from beneath the fabric cornices highlight the red/orange silk and metal organza curtains over the tall windows. A dramatic chandelier drops from the pentagonal-shaped dome cut out of the dropped ceiling in the middle of the room. Here additional seating is provided on armless loveseats and lounge chairs.

Tribeca Grand Hotel, in lower Manhattan, had all of its public spaces designed by Bogdanow Partners Architects of New York. Inspiration for the interior design came from the great Industrial Age interiors and the surrounding architecture of the Tribeca neighborhood.

In the large triangular shaped atrium, designed as an open lobby, there is a lounge, a bar, a waiting room/meeting place and a restaurant. The Church Lounge is located on the first floor of the eight story high atrium and it serves as an alternative to the traditional, formal dining room. The low lounge furniture and cocktail tables are blended with café-style tables and chairs, thus offering guests a choice of seating options. By day, the lounge is "the picture of casual downtown chic" but as night falls "subtle accent lighting and music add to the sensual ambiance of the space."

Featured in the lounge on the reclaimed wood floors is a squared-off, horseshoe shaped bar with a back bar that protrudes into the open rectangular space behind the bar. The back bar has an illuminated display of bottles resting on the mahogany shelves. The lowered ceiling and the upholstered low-back stools all add a cozy, warm and intimate feeling to this area.

In the lounge, barrel-shaped chairs in wine, purple and red upholstery hug round tables. The rich, wood veneered walls are accented with ebony metal strips and sconces with amber glass panels. These sconces "frame" the 16 ft. by 22 ft. "fireplace"—a focal element in the lounge with its 66 paraffin fueled flickering flames.

NORTHERN LIGHTS

STAMFORD MARRIOTT, STAMFORD, CT

DESIGN — *Interior Design Force, New York, NY*
Stephen D. Thompson, ASID: President

PHOTOGRAPHY — *Peter Paige Photography, Upper Saddle River, NJ*

The 2300 sq. ft. Northern Lights serves as a bar/lounge/night-club and it is situated off the main lobby of the Stamford Marriott Hotel in Stamford, CT. The hotel caters to business travelers and local business people and, as designed by Stephen Thompson of Interior Design Force, Inc., the space is a welcoming and comforting oasis in "the eye of the storm."

The challenge to the design team was to turn a dark, depressing and very dated "sports bar" into a modern, multi-functional space that could be an "exciting bar scene" but also be inviting for light lunches, "happy hour," and themed events. "A bright, upbeat atmosphere was desired to make the experience more welcoming to female patrons." The space is raised two steps from the lobby proper and what was previously a multi-level area is now all on one. The ceiling was raised and the structural beams were not only uncovered but they were incorporated into the design. Also revealed were large windows above and below the beams which face the front of the hotel. They are now revealed and covered with sheer curtains. One oversized column became a circular, wood-clad focal point "around which the room revolves." It

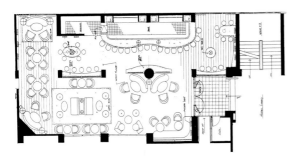

is surrounded by curved, high backed banquettes, round cocktail tables, barrel chairs and majestic high backed pull up chairs,

Between the two newly restored, two story high windows is the long, curvaceous bar. Blue sea glass floats within 3/4 in. thick acrylic panels that are backlit and they serve as the back bar. With ever changing colored lights, "this 'starry night' effect reinforces the Northern Lights theme—as do the custom air-brushed paintings of the aurora borealis." A computerized system of LED light strips changes color through the entire spectrum at any speed or in any combination of colors. "Different customized programs are used to create different moods or to herald a holiday or special event."

According to the designers, "We encouraged our client to try new products, color schemes and styles of furniture as well as a fresh approach to the actual layout, the 'theme' and marketing. We created a sophisticated nightclub, appealing to hotel guests and local patrons, male and female customers. The design is dramatic in daytime as in nighttime. This is a special place to ' see and be seen.'"

LIQUID ASSETS

NEW YORK, NY

DESIGN — *BBGM/Interiors, New York, NY*

ARCHITECT — *Stonehill & Taylor*

LIGHTING CONSULTANT — *Sirmos*

PHOTOGRAPHY — *Courtesy of Hilton Hotels*

The Liquid Assets bar is to be found in the lobby of the Millenium Hilton Hotel in downtown Manhattan. The design by BBGM/Interiors of New York has provided the bar/lounge with seating for 32 on capsule shaped chairs with bent wood arms and on seats upholstered with leather and mohair.

Deep mahogany and ebonized woods blend with the rich aubergine mohair armchairs, the metal accented cocktail tables and the carpeting to affect an air of "low slung, sexy seating." The ebonized face of the bar is accented with a band of sage-colored leather and the bar rests on a black granite tiled floor. The back bar fits into an existing architectural niche and mounted on the backlit green onyx wall are fixed and adjustable shelves. Placed in the bar are long, slim (3 ft. x 9 ft.) light panels covered with silk shades in two tones of amber. "These vertical elements complement the horizontal wood wall paneling and help to define the discreet zones within the overall space." Banquette and bistro seating complete the inviting mix of options for the guests.

Located within a new boutique hotel at 1515 Rhode Island Ave. in Washington, DC, 15 RIA has been designed by Brennan Beer Gorman Monk (BBGM) to "blend seamlessly with the hotel's lobby." It is finished in earth tones and warm woods accented with contemporary metal details.

Leather tiles in chocolate and light caramel colors checkerboard the face of the bar which is topped with Japanese persa granite. Wooden display ledges punctuate the cool slate that runs along the dark walnut back bar. A rounded front cabinet camouflages a TV screen when it is not being viewed.

Small cocktail tables with stools upholstered in a warm terra cotta colored fabric seat the guests in the bar. Others can be seated in a portion of the lobby at small bistro tables and chairs upholstered in a gold on gold patterned fabric and backed with purple velvet. Small loveseats and slipper chairs "with funky geometric patterns" complete the intimate atmosphere.

15 RIA

WASHINGTON, DC

DESIGN — *BBGM/Interiors, New York, NY*

PHOTOGRAPHY — *Tom Crane Photography*

"A contemporary design 'made in Brazil' plus an incredible view of New York" is how Arthur Casas, the designer of the sleek, super-elegant and high styled World Bar described his design. Located in the Trump World Tower in the rapidly regenerating tip of lower Manhattan, Casas and Owen & Mandolfo beat out many leading designers to win this commission.

The two-level space of 280 sq. meters is now a soft, glowing area lightly furnished in a gentle, monochromatic palette from pale creamy beiges to gold with wood accents. All the furniture was produced in Brazil—many from original Casas designs such as the sofas, lounges and armchairs. The unique tall tables that surround the unusually high seating area, constructed around one of the square columns in the space, were designed by Rebellato, a Brazilian artist. In the midst of all the sleek and contemporary furnishings, the bases of these tables seem tree-trunk-like and thus add a rather rustic touch to the scene. The four-sided seating unit has a drink rail set in the floor in front of it for the sitter's comfort. Extending out from the column are metal cylindrical lamps supported by delicate rods. The column helps to support the mezzanine level above which, at this point

WORLD BAR

NEW YORK, NY

DESIGN — *Studio Casas, Sao Paulo, Brazil*
Arur de Mattos Casas — Principal/Designer with
Owen & Mandolfo, New York, NY

PHOTOGRAPHY — *Tuca Reines*

creates a more intimate feeling. The ceiling under the mezzanine is constructed of Canadian wood strips formed into squares and then laid in alternating directions to affect a checkerboard pattern. Other walls and the connecting staircase are also sheathed in this light colored wood.

A long, luminous yellow/gold slab of Calcutta marble serves as the bar. The simple form stretches partially along one of the perimeter walls and another wood clad column

anchors the bar at one end. A 15 ft. mirror serves as the back bar and "reflects all the space and gives a sense of refinement." A similar bar is above on the mezzanine level.

The 40 ft. tall windows that surround the World Bar on two sides offer the fabulous view through the long, sheer drapes that are bottom lit for a spectacular effect of luminescence. With residents in Trump World Tower such as Bill Gates, Sophia Loren, Naomi Campbell and Derek Jeter, Mark Grossich, the owner, said that the World Bar would be much, much more than "some flash in the pan hangout for the trendoids." This is class!

JAZZ CAFÉ

ROME, ITALY

DESIGN — *Studio Ciccotti, Rome, Italy*

PHOTOGRAPHY — *Courtesy of Studio Ciccotti*

Not far from the Piazza Navona—a "must see" stop for tourists to the Eternal City of Rome—is the exciting, color saturated, lounge/bar/café—the Jazz Café. As conceived and created by the designers at Studio Cicciotti—"we wanted to give the mark of a culture to the project—starting with the origin of the café's name, and characterizing each of the furnishing elements with references to music."

Thus, musical themes and symbols appear throughout the space starting with the logo, to the exciting wall mural created by students at Scula Viva, to conga drums that have been converted into bar stools that surround the sweeping

curved bar with the padded leather face. The music bar, notes and clefs that are part of, and follow the curve of the bar top continue, the "melody." This bar is the heart of the space and connects the two ends of the café.

Brick walls and open brick arches separate and yet unify the space with its high, blacked out ceiling and the planked timber flooring. Bright, copper colored HVAC pipes, ducts and vents sweep through the space and outline the U-shaped bar and the frosted cube suspended over it.

Liquor bottles are displayed on the cube which is illuminated from within.

Magenta and red leathers and fabrics are used to upholster the banquettes along the walls and partitions as well as the metal pull-up chairs. Accent lights with red, cerise and orange gels add even more "heat" and excitement to Jazz Café. In the café area two unusual lighting fixtures hang and the rectangular forms are sheets of a musical score—thus adding yet another musical note to the design.

BLUES STATION

COLUMBUS, OH

ARCHITECT — *Cowan Garand Architects,*
Worthington, OH

PHOTOGRAPHY — *Bryan Barr Photography,*
Columbus, OH

Steve Cohee and Mark Stokes, President and VP of Operations of Blue Ventures, wanted to bring a new and different "something" to Columbus' nighttime dining/drinking/entertainment scene—and they did. With the Blues Station "we're bringing Columbus the real thing: great fun in an authentic atmosphere with authentic blues and cuisine."

At 4000 sq. ft. the space is large enough to accommodate a bar, stage and kitchen as well as ample seating. "We looked at a number of downtown and suburban locations and selected this spot because the building and location fits with the blues experience," said Steve Cohee. The design firm of Cowan & Associates of Worthington, OH demolished the building's interior down to its block walls and exposed the ceiling. Reclaimed barn siding—painted black—and corrugated metal are the main wall coverings. Addressing the hard traveled lifestyle and the rhythm of the blues is the full height, interior wall mural of a train and station. The focal stage is treated with faux brick and stucco "to appear as if a brick wall had been covered then exposed by wear and tear of time." The proximity of stage to seating provides this intimate venue with great acoustics. Speaking for the designers, Peter McIntosh said, "There is a connection created from seeing and hearing an act close-up: it's like you personally become part of the scene, a part of the music, a part of the action."

Over the bar, a large metal screen defines the service area and also serves as a display area for merchandising T-shirts and wine. A patio, out back, accommodates outdoor seating and a garage door becomes a pass-through for the bar and also helps to bring the sounds and sights of the live performances out from the inside. The menu features ribs and the "favorite": deep-fried peanut butter and jelly sandwiches.

Blue Ventures is planning to take the show on the road. "In a good music market that has not seen the likes of an authentic blues club like we have developed for Columbus, we feel we will do great."

BB KING DANCE CLUB & NIGHTCLUB

FOXWOODS RESORT CASINO, MASHANTUCKET, CT

DESIGNER — *Yates Silverman, Las Vegas, NV*
Charles Silverman: President
Marge Silverman: VP
Larry Rafferty / Joyce Orias: Project Managers

DESIGN COORDINATOR — *Judd Brown Designs,*
Inc., Warwick, RI
Judd Brown: President
Steven McMahon: VP
Mark Palazio / Timothy Rogers: Project Managers

ARCHITECT OF RECORD — *Jefferson Group*
Architects, Warwick, RI

PHOTOGRAPHY — *Warren Jagger Photography*

The BB King Dance Club and Nightclub are two new additions to the Foxwoods Resort Casino in Mashantucket, CT. The 8300 sq. ft. dance hall is connected to the 4100 sq. ft. nightclub by a backstage walkway that allows performers to share the dressing rooms in the interim space without being seen by the public.

The nightclub was conceived to resemble a renovated warehouse "as a tribute to the homes of the early jazz clubs." Stained concrete floors, exposed brick walls, and an open ceiling grid painted black, evoke a factory feeling. Classic holophone pendant fixtures suspended throughout further reinforce the warehoused/industrial theme. The bar has a hammered copper die while the glowing backlit back bar features a curved glass block wall against which glass shelves are secured. The freestanding tables are accentuated by the

inlay of hands of playing cards with BB King's image on a pair of clubs on the tops.

Sharing honors in the dance club are the backlit, honey-colored onyx bar with its luminous back bar backlit with fluorescent strips and the black granite bar at the opposite end of the space. The eclectic décor includes a multi-color art deco design rug of wheels in motion and coordinated furniture. Art deco moldings enhance the warmly tinted walls. A raised stage set behind a theatrical proscenium is the focal element here and the two-toned wood dance floor, striped in cherry wood and maple, is centered on the stage. The mural surrounding the room is highlighted with special recessed wall washers while other simple recessed lamps supplement the many decorative pendant and sconce lights. Embedded in the movable, polished resin topped tables are graphics of Lucille, BB King's guitar. The chairs and tables can be readily reconfigured as required and for viewing the action on the dance floor.

POWDER

NEW YORK, NY

DESIGN — *Karim Rashid*

PHOTOGRAPHY — *Ramin Talaie, New York, NY*

Brilliant colors—from ruby and poppy red to the complementary chartreuse—to the eye-arresting and restful lavender—all come together in a Chelsea nightclub bar—Powder—as designed by the noted Karim Rashid.

From the non-descript façade of gray stucco one enters into a hallway/staircase of bright hot pink with each step outlined with light. "Amorphous cuts" are what Rashid calls the amoeba shaped cutouts that appear at the top of the steps and throughout the space. These cutouts serve as doorways, windows, visual openings or just to allow light to flow from area to area. Powder is a 20,000 sq. ft. space on one floor plus a mezzanine, and it had to be "visually divided" into smaller, more intimate spaces around the 2500 sq. ft. dance floor. The perimeter seating is raised up around the floor with low vinyl benches with low backs and finished in

purple and orange. Translucent rectangular panels of poppy red glass overlap one another to form a balustrade around the dance floor with the overlaps forming colors within colors. Rashid repeated the same technique around the mezzanine where ruby red glass was used instead of the poppy color. Chartreuse glass topped tables with ribbon-like bases sit between the banquettes that line the walls.

   "Most dance clubs are really dark. I was trying to prove to my client that we could take a light space and using only lighting get it really dark," said Karim Rasahid The pale lavender tinted wall are affected by the colored lights playing upon them and though Rashid used darker colors on the furniture, he used lighting to bring out the original colors of his design. "The easiest thing to do is make everything a perfect box. I need to challenge myself. The overall feeling in architecture is what we're looking for—a humanization of space." To this end the primary walls of the club have no

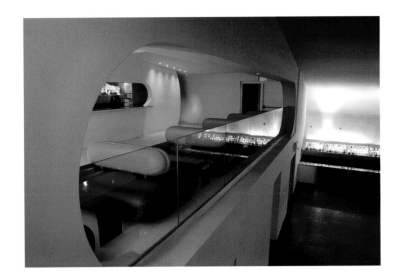

hard corners and when illuminated, the long, uninterrupted wall on the main floor seems to have no edges.

An ovaloid box, on the mezzanine, serves to accommodate the bar. Views to the floor below are visible through cuts in some of the walls. "The amorphous cuts are a way to open one space to another without defining a window." The smaller bar is on the main level and it can be distinguished by a series of assorted vertical cuts above it that light up the drink line. The bars are sheathed in Chromatech—a glass sheeting that refracts colors depending upon the angle and the hue of the lights that hits it—and this provides another source of light for the bar.

"Powder is an inconsistent material. It's merely dust. Everything in the space follows that concept except the furniture, which is very different—square, angular. We wanted the space to be minimal, clean, cold: once it is inhabited, people are what make it warm and inviting."

TABU

DESIGN — *Jeffrey Beers International, New York, NY with Roger Parent*

ARCHITECT OF RECORD — *Youngblood Wucherer Sparer Architects*

PHOTOGRAPHY — *Eric Laignel, Photographer & Patricia Patrinejad, Stylist*

Tabu is a collaborative effort. Gamal Aziz, president of the MGM Grand in Las Vegas wanted "a nightclub venue that catered to an elite, sophisticated crowd and provided an unparalleled combination of service, design and entertainment." Jeffrey Beers of Jeffrey Beers International of New York was immediately brought in for the venture that would be "something sensual, sophisticated and mysterious—but at the same time entertaining." To add the "WOW factor" Roger Parent, the former executive producer of Cirque du Soleil joined Beers and he brought the concept of casting various sensual, intriguing images—mostly the human

body—throughout the space primarily on the bar and table tops. Together they evolved Tabu: "a combination of architectural design genius, creative expertise and surreal artistic interpretation."

There are three diverse rooms. Most of the space is taken up by the major room which features a spirits bar with lighted, revolving liquor towers, reactive tables, private booths slightly inset from the room and separated from the casino by thick frosted glass—and the DJ booth. Roger Parent designed the "animated mural" that runs the full length of one wall and creates a strong visual statement. "The mural is a desertscape featuring faces, images, objects and colored light." The perception of the mural changes depending upon the lighting in the room or which images are being focused on at that specific time. Two reactive/interactive tables (designed by Reactrix Systems) allow guests to manipulate a series of projected images that seemingly bring the table to life.

The Tantra Room is circular in plan and has its own private bar made of ice. The walls are covered with a shimmering fabric and flickering candles are set into niches carved through the room. A hand blown glass and metal pendant fixture hangs overhead and is reflected on the black marble floor. In the rear of Tabu and separated by a wood frame filled with myriad amber resin panels is the Champagne Room. This is a totally private area with purple fabric walls and crystal lighting fixtures. Throughout Tabu, each piece of furniture was especially designed for the space it occupies.

"Tabu combines modern style with sophisticated refinement"—and it is fun!!

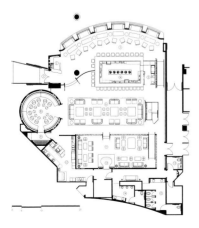

THE PULSE

CRYSTAL SERENITY CRUISE SHIP

DESIGN — *BBGM Interiors, New York, NY*

PHOTOGRAPHY — *Courtesy of Brennan, Beer, Gorman, Monk/Interiors*

"Our goal was to create an environment that is fun, contemporary and slick. Vibrant colors, textures and shapes animate the space and are enhanced by the club's sophisticated lighting system," said Gustin Tan, a design partner at Brennan Beer Gorman Monk (BBGM) Interiors of New York.

Tan is describing The Pulse, a 1300 sq. ft. disco bar on the Crystal Serenity cruise ship that set sail in July 2003. Already the cruise line has been selected by the readers of *Travel & Leisure* magazine as "the Best Large Cruise Ship Line" and The Pulse's 48-seat capacity is always filled!

A passageway line with patterned metal rails leads to The Pulse—"setting the stage for what is ahead." The central focus of the space is the dance floor finished with blue and ivory dimensional, reflective tiles. The dance area is embraced by a semi-circular stainless steel rail at one end and the cylindrical, dark nickel, smoked glass and suede DJ booth at the other end. The rail is topped with black granite and drum-like stools with black leather seats. The drums are wrapped in a bright blue fabric speckled with daubs of primary colors: the same fabric is used on the bar stools. Here dancers can relax and enjoy a drink between sets. Along one of the curved walls that is accentuated with a diamond pattern of metallic strips are sweeping, high backed banquettes, round tables and cube-like chairs.

A stone bar, with an illuminated acrylic front, is backed up by backlit acrylic panels set into the wood veneered wall. Metal and wood shelving span the illuminated areas and the bottles are displayed. The ceiling throughout is blacked out but dropped, sinuous shapes slink and snake overhead and they carry some of the downlights. Blue glass pendants in sets of three mark off each of the banquette seating clusters and dozens of theatrical lighting fixtures fill the black void and provide exciting jolts and blasts of bright color on the dance floor.

"The Pulse has been designed as a sophisticated, fun environment featuring an illuminated bar and wave shaped banquettes."

Rhythm occupies 2500 sq. ft. of the first floor of an existing loft building in the trendy, West Loop part of downtown Chicago. The concept for the bar/disco was inspired by a trip to Capetown, South Africa by the clients/owners Rob and Doug McLennan, where they encountered the communal form of percussion music commonly referred to as a "drum circle": people playing coordinated rhythms. "Rhythm encourages its patrons to actively participate in this experience by providing various percussive instruments and drum lessons for beginners."

RHYTHM

WEST LOOP, CHICAGO, IL

DESIGN — *Aumiller Youngquist, Chicago, IL*
Raymond R. Schaefer, AIA: Principal in Charge
Jonathan Graves: Job Captain

PHOTOGRAPHY — *Mark Ballogg, Steinkamp Ballogg*
Photography, Chicago, IL

As designed by Aumiller Youngquist of Chicago, in response to programmatic requirements and existing spatial conditions, the plan is divided into three areas. Up front are the bar, the stage and a tiered drum pit and dance floor. The rear of the space is divided between a quieter lounge area on one side and bathrooms and service areas on the other. "Conceptually, the bar, lounge, stage and drum circle pit are treated as epicenters of concentric circles emanating from each other. The intersection of these radiating circles influences the forms of the intermediate wood floor insets and defines the general flow through the space."

To convey "the cultural diversity of percussive music and the rhythmic layering," the designers expressed that concept in the interior through the use of ceiling frames and stretched fabric panels that overlay the exposed brick walls and timber ceiling. The warm material and color palette complement the existing wood and brick finishes while spe-

cific details are highlighted with red, yellow and blue colors. The bar area, as an example, is punctuated by backlit colored glass "creating a dynamic backdrop and framing a gong that is used to signal "last call." To create a visually exciting space up front, stained concrete, slatted wood, colored glass and patterned fabrics are combined.

The lounge, in contrast, is softer and quieter in feeling. It is finished with flowing banquette seating, upholstered wall panels, and loose furniture and pillows. Together they "create a more relaxed and subdued ambiance." In total, 180 seated guests can be accommodated.

"The overall design is intended to be evocative rather than literal. Through color, texture, material and form, an atmosphere is created that conveys the essential nature of percussive music and the means in which it is produced. In doing so, Rhythm encourages social interaction and fosters a unique and memorable experience."

DRAGONFLY

HARRISBURG, PA

DESIGN — *Core, Washington, DC*
Peter F. Haspstak, lll, AIA, IDA, ISP
Dale Stewart, AIA
Kathleen Claire Ngiam
Michele LeTourneur / Tomas Quijano

ARCHITECT OF RECORD — *by Design Consultants,*
Camp Hill, PA

PHOTOGRAPHY — *Michael Moran, New York, NY*

What was once a local bank in Harrisburg, PA now houses the 18,000 sq. ft. Dragonfly. With a lounge and bar on the first floor and a VIP lounge and dance floor on the second, Dragonfly is Harrisburg's newest and biggest nighttime "hot spot."

Core of Wasahington, DC was commissioned to "transport party-goers to a place somewhere between Kronenberg meets Mad Max." By using light and simple materials, the designers were able to "alter one's perception of space." The "Pokemon" influence is immediately announced by the colorful, fluorescent lights on the canopy over the entrance into

the gloss white-painted façade of an industrial frame building with Georgian brick styling. "The first image of the club is meant to look otherworldly in an otherwise traditional downtown landscape." The glowing pink and stainless steel "capsule" ticket booth inside "hovers in the low, weathered steel clad entry which gives off a Kool-Ade colored fluorescent back glow." The immense bar, on the first level, is a study of contrasting materials and construction. In this open space elements were added such as the multi-colored light towers and the rippled glass wall panels glowing from the blue, green and lavender fluorescent tubes beside or behind the glass enclosures. The charcoal gray and silver interior is bathed in the colorful illumination and the same cool colors appear on the upholstered lounge chairs which have a decidedly retro 1970's look.

The stairs that connect the two levels are saturated with red, yellow and blue colors and lights. Up on the second level the colors change from cool to hot and hotter. Here the ambiance is fiery and flaming with yellow, orange, red and magenta hues. "The light panels become the key elements to the main dance floor, highlighting silhouettes, while the colored metal panels become the focal elements for the peripheral bars." In contrast to the dim lighting and the plush magenta and tangerine velvet sofas of the VIP area are the long, white cocktail tables that are highlighted by spots in the ceiling.

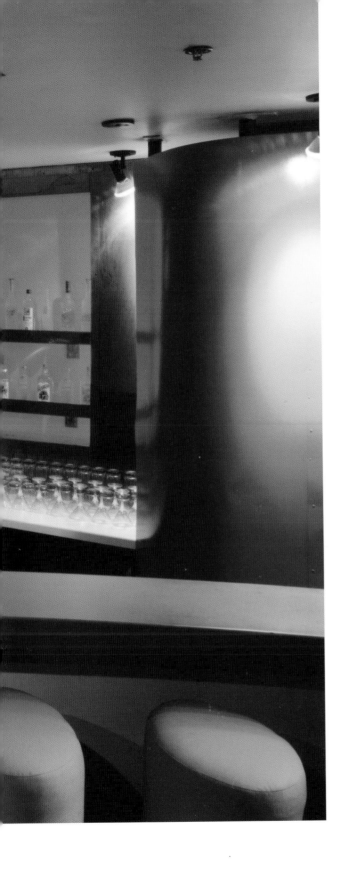

AURA BAR

LONDON, UK

DESIGN — *SSH Architecture & Design Consultants, London, UK*
Graham Harris / Sheridan MacRa / Harley Vincent / Guy Morgan Harris

INTERIOR FINISHES AND FURNITURE DESIGNER — *Steve Crummack*

PHOTOGRAPHY — *Courtesy of SHH*

Aura—voted "London's best new bar" has a fabulous location. It is situated beneath the Caviar House on the corner of St. James St.—in Piccadilly—the heart of London's entertainment scene. Offering pre-war liquors and pre-embargo cigars, Aura communicates "an air of luxurious old world chic" though the design by SHH Architecture & Design Consultants is "cutting edge contemporary." The underground, low-ceilinged space has been transformed into "an

intimate rather than claustrophobic space" with the ceilings painted white and an overall ambiance that suggests "domestic-scale luxury."

The designers used "tricks with perception to dispel any negative feelings of a shut-in space." Art deco style beveled and backlit mirrors appear along the tops of the walls and they are used to encourage or to satisfy the need to "people watch." A leather-lipped, walnut bar—over 30 ft. long—runs along one entire wall. The back bar and the bulkhead over it serve as AV screens upon which are projected old, classic, black and white movies, That also seems to "open up" the space.

In addition to the reclaimed and restored dark timber floors and the mainly chocolate brown covered furniture and the entry's oxblood red walls, the room is colored, re-colored and re-re-colored by the changing colored lights that wash over the already colorful space. Cascading chandeliers drop from raised cutouts in the ceiling to accentuate the luxury attitude of the design. Of special note are the hand crafted, hydraulically re-configurable furniture pieces designed by Steve Crummack. When Aura serves as an upscale restaurant these are low-slung, daytime chairs but they become "lounger beds" when Aura transforms into a "horizontal bar culture" at night.

A DJ keeps the music spinning as the night scene heats up and the changing colors add to the sense of movement and excitement.

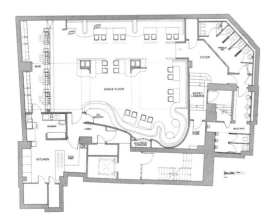

SONOTHEQUE

CHICAGO, IL

DESIGN — *Suhail Design Studio, Chicago, IL*
Suhail: Designer/Principal

PHOTOGRAPHY — *Doug Fogelson*

"DJ driven, jazz based and with options for live shows."
Those were the requirements for Sonotheque and this disco/
lounge/bar was designed by Suhail of Suhail Design Studio
of Chicago. The designer said, "My role was to take this
basic notion and evolve it into a complete environment. The
obvious theme to me was the music but more importantly—
the sound of the space—the acoustics."

Suhail researched the many facets of acoustic design to
affect a space that would be sonically balanced. "This ration-
ale determined the overall look of the space. Wall textures
that responded to various sound frequencies became sculptural architectural wall textures that articulated the surfaces."
A balanced space requires absorption, reflection and diffusion. Snowcrash panels on the lounge walls and acoustic tiles
all on edge and stacked directly above the bar took care of
the "absorption." The custom fabricated, thermoformed
"cityscapes" at either end of the space took care of the
"reflection" while "diffusion" occurred in the ceiling with a
product called Geometrix.

The long, quartz faced bar is located at one side with a
large, low lounge seating area on the opposite wall. "I wanted Sonotheque's design to be detailed by the music. I wanted
the sound to be the color." Thus, the entire design is executed in eight shades of gray—"as representative of the musical
scale" accented by the warm color of the mahogany vinyl
wood lounge area. The ultra-suede low lounge seating is
complemented by the metallic glint of stainless steel. The
high density foam seating also acts as an active reflector for
high frequency sounds. Even the vinyl wood and plastic concrete floor tiles work as reflectors.

"The whole final experience for me," said Suhail, "was
to give the visitor the most beautifully balanced acoustic
sound. But—more than that—I wanted to create a space
that looked the way it sounded."

RAIN IN THE DESERT

LAS VEGAS, NV

DESIGN CONCEPT — *Scott De Graff / Michael Morton: Co-Owners and*
555 Design Fabrication Management, Chicago, IL
James Geier — Principal

PHOTOGRAPHY — *Nine Group*

Rain in the Desert is the unique 25,000 sq.ft. entertainment/bar venue in the Palms Hotel in Las Vegas. Rain in the Desert is built on multiple levels and filled with a variety of environments and visual effects. It combines an electrifying dance club, a stage for headliner performances and a private bar/lounge that can accommodate 75 guests.

One enters Rain in the Desert through a tunnel covered with gold-mirrored mosaic tiles where changing lights, fog and sound "hint at the energy level inside." Inside, ultra-sleek, contemporary furnishings and a palette of red, gold, purple, orange and black combine with materials such as mosaics, terrazzo, glass, and bamboo to create "a dynamic tension and exciting sense of possibility." The stage is flanked by a 16 ft. color-changing, water wall and the stage can also be used as a seating area with bar when there are no scheduled performances.

Circling the perimeter—two levels above the dance floor—are seven "decadent" private cabanas roofed over with adjustable, color-changing awnings. Each cabana can seat eight to 12 guests and each is screened off by beaded curtains. The private booths feature LCDs, programmable mood lighting and specialty furniture. Also on this level is a large bar and a breathtaking view of Las Vegas.

On the mezzanine/VIP level there are six skyboxes with private balconies that overlook the nightclub below. Fifteen to 20 guests can be accommodated in each or the area can be converted into one large, private area for 120 guests. All in all, Rain in the Desert can seat 180 guests.

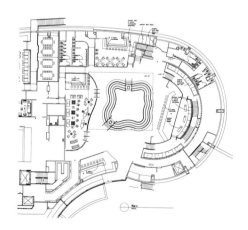

There are six bars in Rain in the Desert and they are all designed with herringbone-patterned fronts of stainless steel and brass. The back bars use various shapes of rear illuminated, glowing panels with floating Plexiglas shelves for the bottle displays. Throughout, the design introduced water elements (rain) into the club and they include the "undulating river with dancing waters" that surround the elevated dance floor and the previously mentioned water walls.

SEVEN

TORONTO, ON

DESIGN — *ll x lV Design Associatesa, Toronto*

PHOTOGRAPHY — *David Whittaker*

Seven is the number of "deadly sins" and that provided the core interior theme for the 6000 sq. ft. bar/lounge located in the heart of Toronto's entertainment district. It is located in an office building where a fourth floor was added onto the original three and connected by an internal staircase. The existing glass curtain wall was replaced with plain dark gray cladding to contrast with the signage: a 40 ft. tall, internally lit, brightly-colored image of numbers falling in perspective down to the simple, horizontal panel that announces the club's name over the doorway. The name is seen, as internally lit, sandblasted lettering on mirrors on the seven landings of the staircase and throughout the facility.

As designed by ll x lV Design Associates of Toronto, the white, stainless steel and glass facility can be changed from a sexy bar/lounge and R&B hot dance destination on weekends to a place for corporate lunches, product launches or fashion shows during the week. A secondary lounge area, on a mezzanine, overlooks the dance floor, the large open lounge and the huge hollow square bar which is lit internally in chartreuse. Four ft. tall, internally-illuminated, column-like drink tables ring the lounge area. The two long perimeter walls back up the white, vinyl upholstered banquette bumper pads with thin back rests that conceal the up-lights that illuminate a line of text sandblasted on the wall-to-wall mirror: "Reason is, and ought to be, only a slave of passions."

The banquette tables are "C" shaped walnut forms and the same shape, in acrylic, appears above the main floor bar for the display of bottles. Walnut is also used for the two story high panel in front of the DJ booth that hovers over the lounge and dance floor. That panel features inset lozenges of stainless steel, "establishing a curving grid pattern

that is deconstructed and elaborated in the dance floor's rear wall and ceiling cladding—custom fabricated vacuum formed Lexan panels into which the theatrical lighting system is integrated." The panels, like the walls, are high gloss white to better reflect and enhance the nightclub lighting effects. The lighting colors play up the "seven deadly sins": lust=blue; pride=violet; envy=green; gluttony=orange; anger=red; greed=yellow and sloth=light blue.

A simple concrete staircase suspended against a full height, gloss finished wall, washed with color, connects the two lounges. The quietly detailed, pure white, low profile furnishings on the mezzanine are accompanied by the same design hollow square bar of the main floor. The 30 ft. inter-

nally-lit bar is backed up by a shallow counter of white epoxy lacquer topped by an integrated stainless drink rail and bottle display that curves up to the ceiling to frame the mirrored wall above. The names of the "sins" are sandblasted into the mirror surface and backlit by continuously changing colored lights. Opposite the bar is a wall with a chartreuse digital supergraphic above a row of long narrow banquette seating.

"Whether bathed In periwinkle, fuchsia or sunset orange light, this remarkable minimalist interior pulsates with personality, in an intimately-scaled, manageable multi-purpose venue that invites guests to explore its possibilities."

TSUNAMI

WEST PALM BEACH, FL.

DESIGN — *GGA (Guillermo Gomez Architect, PC), NY, NY*

ARCHITECT OF RECORD — *Harter Ames*

LIGHTING — *GGA*

PHOTOGRAPHY — *Eric Laignel*

A really big wave of sensational Pan-Asian/ Fusion cuisine has swept over Palm Beach in Florida and it is available at the Tsunami Restaurant of Palm Beach. As designed by Guillermo Gomez of GGA, it is big, dramatic and overwhelming as any good tsunami would be.

In a space of 9000 sq. ft. with ceilings soaring to 29' and windows as tall as 20', the architect/designer has created a dramatic impact with two major spaces or entities. "Both are distinctive and attract different crowds but they are adjacent and connected through this wall that grows up from a contiguous light well and pierces through both spaces". The two areas are the upscale restaurant and the high-energy lounge/ dining room and the spaces are connected by a massive zebrawood-veneered wall. Tsunami also features two bars, an open sushi bar and several private function rooms.

According to Guillermo Gomez, "the space finish provides a Zen-like atmosphere supported with natural materials in a very geometric and minimal way". Though the color palette is mostly neutral, the designer added areas of vibrant color—like the brilliant red wall that encases the golden Buddha—to "create an impact in a subdued atmosphere." Instead of lowering the ceiling in the upscale dining room to "a more human scale", Gomez designed the space with step-up platforms that gradually increase in size. "This allowed for a sense of individuality, a space-within-a-space, all the

platforms united by a majestic light staircase that leads to a
top bar overlooking the main dining room—allowing
patrons to see and be seen".

Lighting played a major role in the design of Tsunami.
Gomez states, "Mostly relying on accent lighting, we proposed an entrance pergola with down light track heads on
the roof that permeate through the trellis work and draw
light slots on the floor". In the entrance area, riverbank
rolling stones camouflage the floor lights that illuminate the
area. To invite diners to step up on the majestic staircase,
there are illuminated nosing edges on the treads and as previously noted, the zebrawood wall "floats on a continuous
light well. The main curved wall in the high-energy lounge
was conceived "as a tremendous light box that reveals the

staggering lights on the wall of the curved corridor leading to the bathrooms.

Tsunami has a maximum occupancy of 400 and can accommodate 170 seated diners, 80 standing at the bar and in the Lounge and 60 out of doors. It has been recognized as one of the top 20 restaurants in Florida.